NEW CENTURY'S
Encyclopaedia of Economics and Commerce

New Century's

Encyclopaedia of

Economics and Commerce

Volume II

(L to Z)

NEW NC CENTURY

New Century Publications

Delhi India

NEW CENTURY PUBLICATIONS
34, Gujranwala Town, Part-2,
Delhi-110 009 INDIA

Tel.: 7138192, 7247805 Tele/Fax: +91-11-7464774
E-mail: indiatax@del2.vsnl.net.in

First Published 2003

ISBN: 81-7708-038-5 (Set)
ISBN: 81-7708-039-3 (Vol. I) ISBN: 81-7708-040-7 (Vol. II)

Published by New Century Publications and printed at Singhal Print Media, Delhi-110 007

PRINTED IN INDIA

Contents

A Note on the Encyclopaedia

Economics and Commerce are the two dominant subjects of modern learning. These are, by no means, easy subjects to master. However, an increasing number of people wish to acquire a working knowledge of economic and commercial terms for use in their daily life.

This encyclopaedia is designed to provide a useful, reliable and readable guide to the fast expanding field of economics and commerce. It contains a careful selection of key terms and concepts in economics and commerce which are considered important for a cross-section of readers including teachers and students of economics, commerce, law and management. This valuable reference work will also be useful for bankers, corporate executives, legislators and government officials. Entries on more technical terms are brief. However, topics of general interest have been explained in the form of essays rather than mere definitions. Both beginners and seasoned professionals will find it full of indispensable facts.

Meticulously cross-referenced, the encyclopaedia is a comprehensive and invaluable source of essential information. Though adequate care has been taken to include in the encyclopaedia as many terms and concepts as possible, a few omissions are likely in this kind of endeavour. The publisher will feel obliged to be informed of such omissions that could find place in the next edition. Similarly, suggestions are welcome to improve the completeness and accuracy of the terms explained in the encyclopaedia.

Thanks are due to the members of the editorial team who all worked tirelessly with their expertise to prepare this encyclopaedia.

Using the Encyclopaedia

The entries in the encyclopaedia are arranged in strict alphabetical order, letter by letter. A complete list of entries is given at the beginning of both the volumes of the encyclopaedia. To make the best use of the material included in the encyclopaedia and also to avoid repetition, entries are elaborately and meticulously cross-referenced in the following manner.

1. Cross-references immediately following an entry either indicate interchangeable terms, e.g. **Floating Debt See Ways and Means Advances** or direct the reader to the relevant description where that particular term is treated as part of a larger entry, e.g. **Open Market Operations See Central Bank**

2. Cross-references at the end of an entry point to the treatment of a related subject explained elsewhere in the encyclopaedia, e.g. **Monopsony:** It is a market situation where there is only one buyer but the number of sellers is very large. See also **Monopoly**.

3. Terms which appear during description of another term and are followed by (q.v.) are entered separately at relevant places in the encyclopaedia, e.g. **Cash Basis Accounting:** Under cash basis accounting, as against **Accrual Basis Accounting** (q.v.), a record is kept of actual receipts (cash incomings) and actual payments (cash outgoings) of a particular year.

An abbreviation is explained in full on its first appearance in each entry.

List of Entries

Volume I

D

Volume II

N

L

Laffer Curve

Named after American economist Arthur Laffer, the curve is used in the context of income tax schedules.

It is argued that at a zero tax rate, no revenue will be collected. Similarly, at a tax rate of 100 per cent, revenue will again be zero because no one would earn taxable income just to pay it to the government. Since tax rates of zero and 100 per cent both raise zero revenue, there must be a tax rate somewhere within that range at which revenue derived is maximum. The curve cannot be a guide to practical policy until one knows where the maximum occurs. Still, the Laffer curve does draw attention to the possibility that reduction in tax rates might yield more tax revenue rather than less.

Lag

Economists often notice a time gap between a cause and its effect. Thus, an increase in money supply (cause) will not increase prices (effect) instantaneously but after a time lag of two or three months. This difference in the period before a cause and effect relationship is established is called lag.

Laissez Faire

It is a French expression, meaning *non-intervention.* To pursue a policy of laissez faire means that the government chooses not to intervene and instead allows ordinary market forces to work themselves out.

Movement for *laissez-faire* was led by British economist Adam Smith (1723-1790) who was motivated by the desire to remove all government controls. He and the other classical economists regarded self-interest as the *invisible hand* which ensured the best functioning of the economy. They regarded governments as necessary evils and advocated minimum functions for them. These functions included defence, law and order and administration of justice. The role of the state was limited to the so-called *police functions*. Beyond these police functions, there should be no attempt on the part of the state to intervene in the functioning of the economy.

However, rapid industrialisation of the 19th century was accompanied by its own problems like unemployment, labour exploitation, economic fluctuations and balance of payment difficulties. State could no longer afford to remain a silent spectator. Faith in automatic price mechanism began to shake and that in intervention started growing. The First World War aggravated the urgency of state interference and the depression of the 1930s proved to be the last straw on camel's back. The whole philosophy of classical economists crumbled down like a house of cards.

From the chaos of depression grew the ideas of British economist John Maynard Keynes (1883-1946). He rejected the normality of full employment hypothesis. On the contrary, he believed that there is generally a discrepancy between demand for and the supply of goods. To restore the balance between the two, a general programme of action is required. The functioning of the price mechanism is imperfect and trade cycles cannot be successfully tackled at the micro-level. Government intervention is necessary to achieve and maintain macro balance in the economy.

Through public work programmes, employment can be raised to a higher level thereby increasing the demand for goods and services. Governments can also influence the level and pattern of production and consumption through fiscal, monetary, trade and industrial policies. Modern governments regulate capitalism through a series of measures which include: (a) minimum wage legislation, (b) mine safety rules, (c) child labour laws, (d) anti-trust legislations and (e) foreign exchange regulations.

Land Cess

It is in the nature of a surcharge on land revenue and is usually collected by the state government along with land revenue and passed on to local bodies.

Landfill Tax

Landfill tax is a fiscal innovation of recent origin, necessitated by world-wide concern for depleting environmental resources. It is a tax on producers who dump their industrial waste in the landfills. It can also be levied on municipal authorities for dumping city waste in the landfills. Such a tax, it is argued encourages recycling and treatment of various types of waste by producers and local authorities. By following proper waste management practices, polluters can avoid the tax and hence contribute to cleaner environment. The tax, thus, acts as a deterrent on dumping industrial and other wastes in the landfills.

The tax may distinguish between active waste and inert waste, the former being more harmful and therefore taxed at a higher rate. For example, in Britain (where the tax was introduced in 1996) active waste is taxed at £10 per tonne as compared to £7 per tonne for inert waste.

Law of Diminishing Returns **See Diminishing Returns, Law of**

Laws of Returns to Scale **See Returns to Scale**

Leads and Lags

This concept is used in the context of short-term capital movements when international payments are accelerated or delayed. When devaluation is feared, importers rush to make payments abroad lest they should pay more after devaluation. This is leads behaviour. However, in a similar situation, exporters will be slow to get their payments from abroad. Foreign companies also delay their payments so as to take advantage of devaluation. This is lags behaviour.

Least Aggregate Sacrifice Principle **See Ability-to-Pay Principle of Taxation**

Leontief's Paradox

Named after Wassily Leontief , it starts from the observation that a country tends to export those commodities which are intensive in the use of that country's relatively abundant factor of production. Conversely, it will import those commodities which are intensive in the use of its relatively scarce factors of production. Since USA is considered to be the most capital-rich country in the world, it is assumed that her exports are capital-intensive and imports labour intensive.

In 1950, Leontief tested this hypothesis on the basis of input-output tables of USA. He found unexpectedly and paradoxically that exports of USA are less capital intensive than her imports i.e. her imports instead of being labour intensive are actually capital intensive. This is known as Leontief Paradox.

This paradox is explained by Leontief with the argument that USA labour is three times more productive than its foreign counterpart. In other words, USA labour force is to be multiplied by three to know its real number. The paradox can also be explained by the commercial policy followed in USA and elsewhere. Restrictions imposed by commercial policies might have influenced trade flows in such a way that the observed factor proportions did not correspond to actual ones.

Letter of Credit

It is popularly known as L/C. It is a document showing promise to pay made by the overseas importer and authenticated by his bank. Thus, the exporter gets security of receiving his export earning. Generally, each L/C contains terms and conditions which need to be clearly scrutinised by the exporter before executing export order.

Letter of credit is of two types, irrevocable and revocable. In the irrevocable L/C, the issuing bank (importer's bank) irrevocably commits itself to make the payment if all the terms are satisfied and all the required documents are presented on or before the due date. A revocable L/C, under which credit can be revoked any time, is not a popular document in trade now.

An irrevocable L/C can be further confirmed by the exporter through his local bank who commits itself to make the payment on presentation of documents. To an exporter, it is an advantage because he will get payment through his local bank. Thus, his risks are localised.

Levy

It is synonymous with tax.

Lien

It refers to the claim of a lender on assets offered as security for a loan.

Life-Cycle Hypothesis **See Consumption Function**

Linear Correlation **See Correlation**

Linear Programming **See Activity Analysis**

Liquidity, International

It is the aggregate stock of assets such as gold, foreign exchange and SDRs held by the national monetary authority and which is available unconditionally to settle the country's imbalance in international transactions. A country's reserve position in the International Monetary Fund is also included herein as it is available for use by the country concerned in the case of balance of payments deficit. The amount of liquidity needed depends on the size and duration of the deficit. The term may be used to refer to the reserves of an individual country or to the sum of reserves of all countries.

Liquidity of an Asset

Liquidity of an asset means how easily can it be converted into cash and at what loss of its capital value. If an asset cannot be converted into cash easily (i.e. at short notice) or at minimum loss of its value, it is less liquid.

Liquidity Preference Theory of the Rate of Interest See Interest

Liquidity Trap See Interest

Loanable Fund Theory of the Rate of Interest See Interest

Local Finance, Principles of

In public finance literature, the following general rules are mentioned as regards financing of local bodies.

1. Where the benefits of a local public service are measurable and accrue to readily identifiable individuals/households within a jurisdiction, user charges are the most appropriate method of financing the service.

2. Local public services which are services to general public in the sense that identification of beneficiaries is difficult, should be financed by taxes on local residents. Such services include traffic control, street lighting, security and general administration.

3. Services the benefits of which spill over to neighbouring jurisdictions should be financed by inter-governmental transfers. These services include health, education, anti-pollution measures and other social welfare activities.

4. Long-term borrowings are the appropriate source to finance infrastructural projects with long-term gains.

Localisation of Industry

It refers to establishment of an industry or cluster of industries in a particular location or region due to availability of cheap factors of production, transport and infrastructural facilities, demand incentives, raw materials etc. These are some of the factors which attract entrepreneurs to set up their plants in a particular area. Once the process starts, it has a tendency to accelerate.

Local Taxation

The term refers to taxes levied at the lower level of government in a federal polity such as municipalities, city corporations, district boards and other local bodies. These local bodies provide certain public services like basic health and education, construction and maintenance of local roads, sanitation, street lighting and parks. Taxes usually levied by local bodies are property tax, octroi, tax on professions and registration and licensing charges.

Lome Treaty

It refers to agreement negotiated in February 1975 between the European Common Market (ECM) and forty-six developing nations, mostly from Africa, Caribbean and the Pacific (ACP) which were former colonies. It came to be known as STABEX Compensatory Financing Scheme. It included a fund to compensate exporting countries in case their prices fall below a stated percentage of the average for the previous three years. It gave duty-free access to the Common Market for all manufactured goods and most farm exports. It also provided for industrial, technical and financial co-operation between ECM and ACP countries.

Long-run **See Short-run and Long-run**

Loss Carry Back

It is a legal provision permitting business assessees to use the operating losses of one year to offset profits of preceding years. Since a business which suffers a loss after having paid taxes in prior years can claim a tax refund after losses appear, such provisions reduce the tax-created risks of business. The time period for which losses can be so carried back is specified in the tax law. See also Loss Carry Forward, and Set Off of Losses.

Loss Carry Forward

A legal provision permitting business assessees to use losses of one year to offset profits of succeeding years.

Under a system of income tax based on net principle, losses of income should attract same considerations as gains. In other words, net gains should attract tax while net losses should be considered for negative tax, i.e. a government refund. In practice, governments do not go so far to help loss-making units but they do provide facilities for carry forward of losses. Loss carry forward (vertical compensation) against future profits amounts to a refund but the taxpayer has to wait for it and this waiting involves loss in terms of interest foregone.

Facility for loss carry forward reduces tax-created risks of business and investment, mitigates disincentive effects of fluctuating incomes, and thereby promotes private enterprise. It can be regarded as a proxy for income averaging provisions. Loss carry forward is a common feature of income tax systems the world over though the number of years allowed for the carry forward differ from system to system. See also Income Averaging; Loss Carry Back; and Loss Set Off.

Loss Set Off

It is a legal provision allowing counterbalancing of losses in one category of activity against profits of another kind of activity within the same taxable year.

In the income tax laws of most countries, income chargeable to tax is computed under different heads. The aggregation of gross total income is relatively easy if income under each head and from each source is positive. However, loss may be sustained in one or more sources under one or more heads of income. Therefore, in the computation of gross total income of an assessee, appropriate adjustments are made of the losses suffered by him. Such adjustments are made in two ways: (a) inter-source adjustment in the same assessment year and (b) inter-head adjustment in the same assessment year. Provisions of (b) are applied only if a loss cannot be set off, fully or partly, under (a).

Loss set off (horizontal compensation) is a common feature of income tax systems the world over though the conditions for it differ from system to system. See also Loss Carry Back; Loss Carry Forward; and Income Averaging.

Lump Sum Tax

It refers to taxation of income, net wealth etc. expressed as a certain fixed sum rather than calculated under the ordinary tax law. This method is used for administrative convenience where facts are difficult to establish. In a lump sum tax, an individual cannot take action to alter his tax liability.

M

Macroeconomics and Microeconomics

Economic analysis has two phases: macroeconomics and microeconomics. Macroeconomics or aggregative economics is the study of the economy as a whole. It examines factors which govern the aggregate size of the economy. Thus, it deals with such variables as national income, total consumption, general price level and total exports and imports of a country.

Microeconomics is that part of economic analysis which examines particular components of the national economy. It studies adjustments of the various parts of the economy in detail. Thus, it includes the study of consumer behaviour, equilibrium of a firm, pricing of a product, pricing of a factor of production, location of an industry, choice of technology and exports and imports of individual items.

Whether an economic phenomenon is macro or micro depends upon the definition of the whole. In the context of the formulation of world economic model, the study of the Indian economy would be micro in nature. Both macro and micro economic concepts are complementary to understand the working of an economy.

Managed Float

Managed float (also called dirty float) refers to floating exchange rate system in which government intervention takes place secretly. Overtly, the government maintains that it is the demand and supply forces which determine exchange rate but secretly it may ask the central bank to intervene in the exchange market to stabilise the currency at the desired level. International Monetary Fund has developed some guidelines for such interventions, and named this system as managed float. It is a device to correct disequilibrium in the balance of payments.

Marginal Cost See Cost of Production

Marginal Efficiency of Capital See Absorptive Capacity

Marginal Propensity to Consume See Propensity to Consume

Marginal Propensity to Import (MPM)

It refers to change in imports as a ratio of change in total domestic expenditure. For example, if total domestic expenditure goes up from Rs. 1,000 crore to Rs. 1,250 crore and imports go up from Rs. 800 crore to Rs. 900 crore, then MPM = 100 ÷ 250 = 0.4

Marginal Rate of Substitution (MRS)

It is the amount of one commodity which must be given up in order to consume an additional unit of another commodity so that the total utility received from both the commodities remains constant. It is shown with the help of consumption indifference curves.

Marginal Rate of Transformation (MRT)

It is the amount of one commodity which must be given up in order to produce an additional unit of another commodity. It is shown with the help of Production Isoquants (q.v.) or production indifference curves.

Marginal Revenue See Revenue

Marginal Rule

Profit maximisation is the objective function of a firm. What should be the level of a firm's output so that profit is maximised? This question is answered with the help of marginal rule. If at the present level of output a firm finds the cost of making another unit (marginal cost) less than the revenue gained by selling that unit (marginal revenue), total profit can be increased by producing the additional unit. Therefore, whenever a firm finds that marginal revenue exceeds marginal cost, it must expand output to increase profit. Conversely, if the firm finds that the cost of producing the last unit of its current output exceeds the revenue gained by selling it, total profit can be increased by not producing the last unit. Thus, whenever marginal cost (MC) exceeds marginal revenue (MR), a firm can increase profit by contracting output.

In short, a firm should change its output whenever marginal cost is not equal to marginal revenue. According to marginal rule, a firm should raise output if MR exceeds MC and lower it if MC exceeds MR. It follows that at the profit-maximising output MR=MC. This is shown by point E in the Figure below.

The equality of marginal cost and marginal revenue is necessary but not sufficient for profit maximisation. In the Figure below, there are two output levels where MC=MR (points E and E'). These two points represent entirely different situations: point E showing maximum profit while point E' depicting minimum profit. Since we are interested in maximum profit situation, we add another condition to the marginal rule. Geometrically, this condition states that at the profit maximising output, the marginal cost curve should intersect the marginal revenue curve from below (as is the case at point E in the Figure).

When the firm has chosen its profit-maximising output (or optimum output), it achieves equilibrium. It has no incentive to increase or decrease output from this equilibrium level. The marginal rule of profit-maximisation is applicable not only to perfect competition but to all types of market situations.

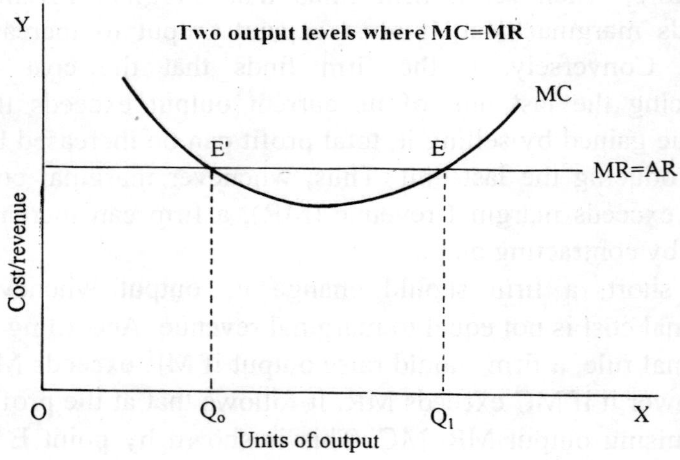

Marginal Tax Rate

It is the rate of tax, under a progressive rate schedule, applicable to the top slice or bracket of an assessee's income, net wealth or some other taxable item.

Market

In economics, market is defined as an area over which buyers and sellers negotiate the exchange of a specified commodity (sugar, wheat, crude oil, gold). The buyers and sellers must be able to communicate with each other and make meaningful deals over the whole market.

Market Capitalisation

It is the value of a company calculated by multiplying the price of its shares on the stock exchange by the number of shares issued.

Market Mechanism

It is an economic system to allocate resources among various lines of activity. It also adjusts production and consumption, distributes income and brings about economic growth. Market mechanism (also called price mechanism) operates when the following three conditions are met: (a) individual economic units decide themselves what, how and when to produce, (b) they do so largely with reference to prices in the broadest sense of the word and (c) prices respond to the forces of demand and supply for the individual goods or factors. The end result tends to be the equilibrium of demand and supply.

Market mechanism, or what Adam Smith (1723-1790) called *invisible hand,* directs and co-ordinates the decisions and activities of millions of independent, dispersed economic units. With all its problems and imperfections, it is surely one of the most remarkable of social institutions. The adjustment to disturbances in a market economy is automatic. Shortage of a commodity in relation to its demand brings about a rise in the price of the commodity.

The price rise then acts as a signal to buyers to use less of it. It is also a signal to producers to shift more resources to its production because it is more profitable to produce it. This then is a case of automatic adjustment or self-regulation. A market economy is a decentralised system in comparison with a command economy.

Market Structure

Market structure means the type of market in which a firm operates. The number of buyers and sellers, and the nature of the product traded are important characteristics of market structure. Perfect Competition (q.v.) and Monopoly (q.v.) are the two extreme market situations. In between these two extremes lie a number of other market structures such as Monopolistic Competition (q.v.), Oligopoly (q.v.) and Duopoly (q.v.). All these in-between market structures are collectively called Imperfect Competition (q.v.).

Marshall-Lerner Condition

It states that devaluation of currency improves the balance of payments position of a country if the sum of the elasticities of exports and imports is greater than unity.

Marxism

During the early stages of the evolution of capitalism (late 18th and early 19th centuries), the condition of the working class was very miserable. Wage-earners had to do long hours of work under unhygienic conditions and without any social security cover. The exploitation of the proletariat (workers) under capitalism led to the writings of Karl Marx (1818-1883), a German philosopher with revolutionary zeal. He published two epoch-making works in collaboration with his friend and benefactor Friedrich Engels (1820-1895): *The Communist Manifesto* (1848) and *Das Capital* (1867). These two works immensely influenced the thinking of the contemporary world.

According to Marx, economic events are dominant in controlling the political and social life of man. This he called the materialistic interpretation of history. Marx saw in the capitalistic system certain forces at work which would cause its demise. He predicted inevitable self-destruction of capitalism due to its inherent contradictions. By paying labour a subsistence wage which was less than its full value, capitalists received a profit. This unearned increment was termed surplus value, i.e. the difference between what workers produced and what they were paid.

Marx believed that the advantages of large-scale production would ultimately lead to concentration of industry in the hands of a few powerful capitalists. The rest of the society would be forced into the position of miserable wage-earners. The wages would go down to the barest minimum owing to pressure of population and the exploitation by the capitalists. At the same time, capitalists would be left with surplus of wealth, much more than they can use for their own enjoyment. They would invest this surplus with the result that there would be excess of production than what the wages of the workers can buy. The over-production and hence the unsold products of the capitalist system would cause depressions, leading to its collapse eventually due to its internal contradictions. Workers, if organised, could take advantage of this catastrophe and set up a collectivist society. In such a society, the capitalists would be dispossessed of their wealth, and industry would be owned and operated by the organised workers for their own benefit. Since this prediction was based on scientific line of reasoning, Marxian system is sometimes called *scientific socialism* by his supporters.

Most of Marx's work consisted of a critique of capitalism which, he believed, was fundamentally an act of robbery. On what was to come, Marx was less precise. The notion of dialectical materialism constitutes the basis of Marxian philosophy. It lays emphasis on change inherent in the material and physical environment of societies. Just as feudal societies were reformulated into the market system, Marx saw as inevitable further changes in economic, social and political spheres. The theory which maintains that there is a pattern of regularity in social development is called *the materialistic interpretation of history* or historical materialism.

Mean

In case of individual observations, mean (i.e. arithmetic mean) is calculated by adding together the various values of the variable and dividing the total by the number of items. For example, the arithmetic mean of the numbers 8, 3, 5, 12, 10 is 38/5 = 7.6.

Median

In statistics, the median of a set of numbers arranged in order of magnitude is the middle value. It is, thus, a positional average. For example, the set of numbers 3, 4, 4, 5, 6, 8, 8, 8, 10 has median 6. Similarly, the set of numbers 5, 5, 7, 9, 11, 12, 15, 18 has median 1/2 (9+11) = 10.

Mercantile Method of Accounting **See Accrual Basis Accounting**

Mercantilism

The term refers to a pre-classical school of thought believing in a commercial policy under which generation of stock of precious metals like gold and silver through an export surplus was the main objective. This school strongly supported tariffs, quotas, embargoes, colonialism and strict navigation laws and above all corn laws to build up national political and military power. Classical economists like Adam Smith (1723-1790) and David Ricardo (1772-1823) did not approve of these restrictive ideas and instead advocated competition and free trade.

The policy of mercantilism was pursued by almost all European countries in the 17th and early 18th centuries to increase wealth and power by encouraging export of goods in return for gold.

As a school of thought, mercantilism advocated commercialisation and industrialisation as key objectives of economic policy of a nation. The mercantilists developed the balance of payments concept primarily because they considered it in the national interest to overbalance imports with exports and thus to acquire precious metals.

Pursuing the mercantilist approach, individual governments in Europe promoted large investments in export industries; built high tariff walls to restrict imports which could be produced domestically; restricted exports of domestic raw materials which could be used by the domestic industry; interfered with the emigration of skilled workers; encouraged immigration of skilled workers; and, in several cases, prohibited sales of precious metals to foreigners.

Under mercantilism, one country's gold gain almost always resulted in a gold loss to one of its trading partners. Hence, all nations could not succeed at the same time. This resulted in sharpened trade rivalries. When successful, mercantilist policies generally resulted in full employment of a country's resources and led to rapid economic growth.

Merchant Bank

It is a financial institution which performs a wide range of activities including advising companies on take-overs, amalgamations, flotations and share issues.

Merchant Marine

It refers to a country's shipping capacity engaged in trade and measured in terms of number and types of vessels.

Microeconomics **See Macroeconomics and Microeconomics**

Minimum Alternative Tax (MAT)

Income tax laws throughout the world generally provide for a number of tax concessions. A clever profit-making company may arrange its affairs in such a manner that the cumulative effect of all tax concessions is to reduce its income declared in the tax return to zero. MAT is a device to keep a Zero Tax Company (q.v.) within the tax net.

In India, if the income disclosed by a company in the tax return (after claiming all deductions) is less than 30 per cent of its book profits then this 30 per cent of the book profits is subject to tax.

The concept of minimum alternative tax also prevails in the United States where it is called Alternative Minimum Tax (AMT). However, under its laws if in the subsequent years the company pays tax on its regular income (income declared in the tax return) then the minimum alternative tax paid earlier on its adjusted taxable income is allowed as a set off against the tax payable on regular income.

In USA, AMT was designed as a part of the Tax Reform Act of 1986, in response to the concern that a number of firms that reported positive book profits paid no corporate tax to the Federal Government.

Mint Parity **See Gold Standard**

Mixed Economy

A mixed economy is one where capitalism and socialism coexist. In the real world, there are no purely capitalist or socialist economies. Even in USA, some buildings, equipment and machines are owned by the government. Contrarily, in a socialist state some small farms or shops are owned by private individuals. Strictly speaking, every economy of the world is a mixed economy. The important thing is the degree by which an economic system is diluted by a different form of economic organisation. In USA, the dilution of capitalism is very less while it is quite significant in India. Indeed, a good example of a mixed economy is provided by India where Government owns a substantial part of the resources, particularly in the industrial sector.

Mixed Income of Self-employed

It is not always that a person serves as an employee. In most cases people work for themselves and so they are described as self-employed. They use their own labour and property instead of lending them to others. They are producers in their own right. Income of such self-employed persons is called mixed income because it is a mixture of rent, interest, wages and profits. The income of a private medical practitioner is mixed income while a doctor serving in a hospital gets wages. It is difficult to segregate the labour and property income of a private medical practitioner. Thus, whatever surplus is available to him after deducting intermediate consumption is treated his mixed income.

Mode

In statistics, the mode of a set of numbers is that value which occurs with the greatest frequency, i.e. it is the most common value. For example, the set of numbers
2, 2, 5, 7, 9, 9, 9, 10, 10, 11, 12, 18 has mode 9.

Mode of Production

Production relations connected with a given type of ownership of the means of production are jointly called mode of production. It is the ownership of the means of production which decides the manner in which they are used. The ownership of the means of production forms the foundation and the organisational principle of production and distribution relations.

If the means of production are socially owned, they become the common property of all the members of society. Private property may be owned by individuals or groups of individuals like the shareholders of a company. However, such groups do not include all the members of a given society. Some forms of property occupy a half-way position, being neither purely social nor purely private such as property of a co-operative society which embraces only part of the members of a given society.

A study of the historical development of human society enables us to distinguish five basic modes of production which roughly coincide with certain periods of human history.

Primitive Community: In this mode of production, the means of production (chiefly land) are the common property of the community.

Slavery: In this system, both the means of production and those who use them are the property of others (i.e. slave owners). Slaves can be either private property or they may be the property of the state (i.e. of a monarch).

Feudalism: Under it, land is partly private and partly state (royal) property. It may also belong to associations like a church. Those who till the land are attached to it as serfs and cannot leave it at will. The land owners allot them plots of land for their personal use and in return they are obliged to till the landowners' fields. The serfs also pay, as tribute to the feudal lords, a part of the produce of the land allotted to them.

Capitalist Production: This is the fourth mode of production under which production takes place for exchange. The means of production are the property of a certain section of society, the capitalists. The rest of the members of such a society do not possess their own means of production. They work as free wage-labourers, operating the means of production owned by the capitalists. The capitalists own the means of production either individually or corporately. This kind of production is characterised by large production units where large number of hired workers are employed.

Socialist Production : In this case the means of production are the property of the whole society. Under certain conditions, part of the means of production may be jointly owned by co-operative associations or municipalities or rural communities. The production process is consciously planned and directed by society in order to satisfy the needs of all its members.

The five modes of production described above roughly correspond to certain periods in the historical development of mankind. Between these periods there can be transitional stages when two or more different modes of production exist side by side. For example, under capitalism elements of feudalism have survived in many countries.

Apart from these five modes of production, there is also another which continually appears as a subsidiary mode of production, viz. *simple commodity production*. Under it, the means of production are the private property of the producers who themselves use them and exchange their products for the products of other producers.

The modes of production specified above can be classified into two types according to their production relations. In one type of production relations all members of society share in the ownership of the means of production. This is the case when the means of production are socially owned as, for example, in the *primitive community* and in the *socialist mode of production*. The situation would be similar in the case of simple commodity production should it ever dominate society. These are, therefore, the cases of *non-antagonistic* modes of production.

In the second type of production relations not all members of society share in the ownership of the means of production. For example, slaves do not own any means of production. Serfs own no land. Under capitalism, hired labourers use the means of production owned by the capitalists. In all these modes of production, the ownership of the means of production is the privilege, or the monopoly of one part of society only. In such a case, the society is divided into *social classes* and production relations are *antagonistic*.

Modern Theory of Rent See Rent

Monetarism

It stresses the role of money supply in determining the level of various important variables in the economy. Excess supply of money in an open economy translates into excess demand for goods and services which in turn gets reflected in an excess of imports over exports until the excess supply of money has gone abroad. Alternatively, the excess demand for goods can lead to rise in prices.

Monetary Policy

Monetary policy refers to the expansion or contraction of money and credit supply in an economy. Since monetary policy includes the regulation of both the volume and allocation of credit therefore credit policy is a part of the overall monetary policy.

Monetary policy operates through changes in the stock of money and changes in the cost and availability of credit. The operation of monetary policy rests on the interrelationship between the stock of money, output and prices. Through money creation, credit is made available to productive enterprises. The availability of credit has favourable impact on output. Simultaneously, increase in money supply raises demand, exerting pressure on prices. The output effect and the price effect must be considered together to assess the overall effect of a monetary measure on the economy.

Objectives of Monetary Policy: Monetary policy is of crucial importance in the context of the overall development of a country. The objectives of monetary policy are, by and large, the same as those of general economic policy.

Price stability is of prime concern for a developing country like India. The term price stability is not used here in a rigid sense to mean price fixity. A modest increase of 2 to 3 per cent in price level per annum is compatible, sometimes even desirable, with the general connotation of price stability. Since price rise is closely linked with the supply of money therefore monetary policy holds the key to price stability. This is why the economists stress growth with stability as the ideal objective of economic policy of a country.

Many developing countries suffer from chronic deficits in their trade balances. This is so because their imports exceed exports. Since imports are essential for the development of the economy therefore it is necessary to increase exports to pay for imports. Domestic price stability is a precondition for increasing exports. Monetary policy becomes relevant in this connection.

Rapid economic development is another concern of policymakers in developing countries. All policies of the Government, including the monetary policy, are geared to achieve this objective. The need for monetary resources is linked with the increase in output and the desire for investment. Monetary policy should react to such changes in time and adequately. It should ensure proper balance between the monetary needs of the economy and money supply. Monetary policy, by influencing the cost, volume and direction of credit, contributes to the achievement of general objectives of economic policy.

Monetary Policy and Fiscal Policy: Monetary policy and Fiscal Policy (q.v.) are two important instruments of the general economic policy of a government. Monetary policy and fiscal policy affect the economy in different ways. Fiscal policy is more direct in its effects. It straightway determines government expenditure and affects private expenditure through taxation measures. Fiscal policy, through budgetary deficits or surpluses, determines changes in government debt and hence issue of new currency. Contrarily, monetary policy has no direct spending and income effects. The effects of monetary policy are indirect and depend on the reactions of lenders and borrowers to the changes brought about by monetary policy. Changes in the monetary policy are more frequent and can be made at any time during a year. However, changes in fiscal policy are less frequent and may require parliamentary approval.

Money

Under a system of simple commodity production, exchange of goods was accomplished largely through barter. The main difficulty of the barter system was the double coincidence of wants. In a modern economy, characterised by acute specialisation and exchange, barter system would just be impossible. It is, therefore, necessary to accept some one thing as a medium of exchange. Any generally accepted thing which serves as a medium of exchange may be called money. Historically, a variety of things have served as money including goats, coins, paper currency and demand deposits of banks.

Kinds of Money: Money may be in the form of some commodity (goat, silver etc.) or merely a nominal unit of account like paper money. These days three kinds of money is important, viz. coins, paper currency and bank deposit money. Coins are example of metallic money. Their intrinsic value is less than their face value and therefore they are not full-bodied but only token money.

In modern times, paper currency has replaced metallic money. Paper money is accepted by the people readily in all kinds of transactions. This is so because government makes it legal tender. In other words, it circulates by command (fiat) and therefore is called *fiat money.*

Deposit money denotes bank deposits against which cheques can be drawn. Normally, demand deposits are taken into account for this purpose. Deposit money is not a legal tender like currency notes. Because it circulates by trust commanded by its issuers therefore it is often called *fiduciary money.*

Functions of Money: The first and the most important function of money is to act as a medium of exchange. As a matter of fact, money is defined in terms of this unique function. Other functions of money are more or less derived from this function. By using money as a medium of exchange, a society can get rid of the difficulties of barter system. By the use of money, exchange becomes easy and this promotes specialisation which has its own advantages in a modern society.

Money serves as a unit of account or standard of value. Money is used to express and compare the values of goods and services which enter the market. Values of goods and services when expressed in terms of money are called prices. With the help of these prices, the ratio of exchange between any two commodities can easily be determined. As a measure of value, money helps us to know almost instantly how much sugar is worth how much butter.

Unfortunately, money as a standard of value is not fixed but a variable one. This is so because the value of money, i.e. the purchasing power of money itself changes from time to time in view of the changes in the general level of prices. The same ten rupee note purchases different quantities of sugar at different times. It is like measuring cloth with a rubber meter the length of which varies with stretching efforts. This instability in money as a standard of value can cause great turmoil in the economy. It is interesting to note that in measuring weight, length and time man has devised invariable units, namely kilogram, metre and minute which are fixed over time and across regions. However, a fixed measure of value is yet to be achieved.

Money serves as a measure of deferred or future payments. These deferred payments pertain to debts and interest thereon, insurance premiums and future instalments of goods purchased at present. The agreements of deferred payments are in terms of money the value of which is subject to fluctuations. Therefore, money is an imperfect standard of deferred payments also. This attribute has serious repercussions for debtors and creditors.

Money also serves as a store of value. People find it easy to hold some of their wealth in money form rather than in terms of commodities. Value can, of course, be stored in terms of other assets but they are not as readily acceptable means of payment as money. However, variations in the value of money cause disturbances in its role as a store of value as in the case of its function as a measure of value and as a standard of deferred payments.

Money Cost **See Cost of Production**

Money Illusion

It arises when a person associates money directly with its face value without considering its purchasing power. If wages of a worker are doubled when prices double, his real wages remain constant. However, if the worker feels better off after the wage hike, he suffers from money illusion.

Money Interest **See Interest**

Money Wages **See Wages**

Monopolistic Competition

Perfect competition and monopoly are two extreme market situations. In the real world, most firms operate under intermediate market structures like oligopoly, duopoly and monopolistic competition. These intermediate market structures are collectively called *imperfect competition.* Monopolistic competition is the most representative example of *imperfect competition.*

In perfect competition, firms sell a homogenous product and face a market price which they cannot influence. In monopolistic competition, firms sell differentiated products as, for example, different brands of soap, toothpaste and soft drinks. Though a firm is not a monopolist of a product as such yet it is the only producer of a particular brand of that product. Various brands of a product produced by different firms are close substitutes but not exactly alike. A producer in such a market has close rivals. Therefore, the market is competitive as well as monopolistic. It is competitive because there are rivals; it is monopolistic because each firm has monopoly over its own brand of the product. Since a firm is the only producer of its own brand of the product, it can exercise some control over its price. In other words, a firm is not a price-taker (as in perfect competition) but a price-setter.

Monopoly

Monopoly is a market situation characterised by one seller and many buyers. It is the opposite extreme of perfect competition. Being the sole seller, a monopolist has the power to influence the market price. Unlike a competitive firm, a monopolist firm is a price-setter, not a price-taker. Since a monopolist is the only producer of his product, the distinction between a firm and the industry vanishes. Thus, a monopolist faces the usual downward sloping market demand curve which is also his average revenue curve. He can choose any price-quantity combination on this curve.

Monopoly may arise due to any of the following reasons: 1. A firm may control the entire supply of raw materials needed to produce the commodity. 2. A firm may own a patent which prohibits other firms from producing the same commodity. 3. A monopoly may be established by government order. 4. Increasing returns to scale in a firm may operate over a sufficiently large range of output so that only one firm is left in the industry.

Price Discrimination or Discriminating Monopoly: Price discrimination occurs when a monopolist sells different units of his output at different prices. There are two types of this discrimination: (a) Discrimination among units sold to the same buyer as, for example, offering the first shirt at full price and the second for only half price. (b) Discrimination among buyers as, for example, a doctor charging more fee from a rich patient and less fee from a poor patient for the same services.

If a monopolist can discriminate among units sold, he can always earn a higher total revenue than by charging a single price. In other words, price discrimination is always advantageous to the monopolist. This is so because price discrimination allows the monopolist to capture some of the consumer surplus which would otherwise go to the buyers.

Conditions for Price Discrimination: Price discrimination is always profitable for the monopolist. However, there is a basic condition if price discrimination is to succeed. Successful price discrimination requires that goods cannot be resold by the buyer who faces lower price to the buyer who faces higher price. The ability to prevent resale depends on the following factors.

1. It is associated with the character or the nature of the product traded. It is fairly easy to resell movable commodities like sugar, butter and milk. However, it is pretty difficult to resell those goods which are installed like sanitary and electrical fittings. The resale of direct services like a haircut is impossible. That is why price discrimination is more successful in case of direct services.

2. Resale may not take place owing to consumers' peculiarities. For example, buyer A may be unaware that buyer B is paying a lower price for the same commodity. Similarly, if price differences are very small, buyers may just ignore them.

3. Resale will be difficult when consumers are separated by distance. Clearly, so long as the transportation cost is more than the price differential, resale will not be profitable. Apart from geographical barriers, resale may be prevented by artificial barriers like tariffs and import quotas. Duties on imports into a country would allow a monopolist producing in that country to charge a higher price in his home market.

Is Price Discrimination Desirable? There is no straight answer to this question. Whether price discrimination is good or bad depends on the merit of the case. It is also a matter of value judgement.

It is wrong to suggest that price discrimination is always undesirable because situation may arise justifying discrimination. In a college, students belonging to rich families are charged full fee, others pay half-fee and poor students are exempted from paying fee. Certainly, discrimination is preferable to non-discrimination in this case. There is nothing in economic theory to suggest that price discrimination is undesirable. See also Monopsony.

Monopsony

It is a market situation where there is only one buyer but the number of sellers is very large. For example, owner of a sugar mill in a remote area is the only buyer of the labour services of the inhabitants of that area. See also Monopoly.

Most Favoured Nation Clause (MFNC)

MFN clause is at the heart of modern commercial diplomacy. Under it, parties give each other all of the concessions which they give to any other country.

The nomenclature is somewhat misleading as it sounds like a promise of preferential treatment. Instead, it is a promise that *no other country* will be given preferential treatment. In other words, the partner will receive treatment no less favourable than that given to any other country.

For example, if country A grants tariff concession to country B, then it must also extend it to all other countries. This extension of concession can be conditional, i.e. other countries must also reciprocate with similar concessions. But it can also be unconditional, i.e. without there being any reciprocity. Such a case is rare these days. Exceptions to MFN clause occur when a country is a member of a Customs Union (q.v.) or Free Trade Area (q.v.) where non-members are not given tariff exemptions.

Motor Vehicle Tax

It is a tax on vehicles suitable for use on roads. It is levied for granting registration, permit, driving licence etc., and is based on the type of vehicle (truck, bus, car, or scooter). It also means a tax paid periodically for the use of roads. Hence, it is also called road tax.

Multicollinearity

In multiple regression, the presence of any fixed relations between independent variables poses the problem called multicollinearity.

Multilateral Aid See Foreign Aid

Multilateral Double Tax Conventions See Double Tax Treaty

Multilateral Trade Negotiations (MTN)

It is a situation in which more than two countries are involved in trade negotiations.

Multinational Corporation

A multinational corporation (MNC) or transnational corporation is a large sized, dominant company involved in production and trade of a wide range of commodities or services and based in two or more countries. It consists of a parent company from where it emerged and where its ownership and management rest. In other countries, there are subsidiaries which are partly owned and managed by people of various nationalities. Large capital base, technological superiority, innovations, advertisements and an oligopolistic ownership have led to the growth of transnational corporation since the early 1960s.

MNCs exercise managerial control over operations in more than one national market. What constitutes managerial control is a debatable topic involving political, legal and economic issues.

Considerable controversy exists as to the economic and political consequences of the existence of multinational corporations. For example, there is a view that the presence of subsidiaries of multinational firms have insidious effects on the economies of developing countries.

There is also a view that multinational corporations act against the interests of home countries (countries in which MNCs are headquartered). It is argued, particularly by trade union leaders that overseas activities of MNCs serve to transfer technology and increase their profits at the expense of job opportunities and income for domestic labour.

Yet another view is that MNCs generate net economic benefits for home and host countries alike.

Multiple Correlation **See Correlation**

Multiple Regression

Economic relationships involve variables. The cases for which there is truly only a single causative factor are few and far between. In real life, causes responsible for a particular happening are multiple and often interconnected.

For example, demand for sugar is a function of its price and income of the consumer. When three or more variables are involved, the least-square estimate of a function is called multiple regression equation. See also Regression.

Multiplier

It is the numerical relationship between a given increment in investment and the resultant increase in national income. An increase or decrease in investment effects a change in total income. Multiplier measures the amount of this effect. It states that an addition to investment will increase the national income by a greater amount - a multiplier of itself.

Suppose a given increment of new investment (say Rs. 10,000) is injected into the circuit flow of money. This is paid out by business firms/government to factor suppliers. A part of it is spent for consumption goods and the rest is saved. The part that is spent for consumption flows down through the circuit to the business firms that produce consumption goods for the market, and is again paid out by these firms to the suppliers of factors employed to produce more goods for consumers. If the recipients of the initial Rs. 10,000 of investment spend 2/3 of it in consumption, i.e. their Marginal Propensity to Consumption (q.v.) is 2/3, Rs. 6,667 will go through the circuit in this second round. The recipients of this Rs. 6,667 will again spend a part of it, and save the remainder. Assuming their marginal propensity to consume is also 2/3, then Rs. 4,444 will go down through the circuit in the next round. If this exercise is repeated indefinitely, it will give the series: Rs. 10,000 + Rs. 6667 + Rs. 4444 + Rs. 2952 + ... in which each item is two-thirds of its predecessor. Mathematically, it can be demonstrated that the sum of this series is Rs. 30,000 which is three times the amount of the initial investment. Then, in this case the value of multiplier is 3. National money income has increased by three times the amount of the new investment.

The value of the multiplier depends on the marginal propensity to consume (MPC). If it is 2/3, the value of multiplier will be 3. If MPC is 4/5, the multiplier will be 5. The mathematical formula for computing the multiplier (K) is

$$K = \frac{1}{1 - MPC}$$

In the extreme case where marginal propensity to consume is zero, the value of multiplier is 1. Contrarily, if the marginal propensity to consume is 1, the value of multiplier is infinite. In practice, the MPC is greater than zero but less than 1.

$0 < MPC < 1$

The value of multiplier is high in underdeveloped countries because MPC of the people is high.

Multiplier-accelerator Theory

It states that business cycles in an economy are caused by the interaction of the multiplier and the accelerator. See also Accelerator Principle; and Multiplier.

N

National Accounting **See National Income**

National Capital **See National Wealth and National Capital**

National Income

The purpose of economic activities going around is to produce goods and services to satisfy the wants of the people. How well and to what extent these wants are satisfied can be known by measuring the total output of goods and services in a country during a specified period. This is the subject-matter of the study of national income.

National income is one of the various macroeconomics aggregates described and estimated under the general heading *national accounting*. Thus, national accounting is a much broader concept encompassing the estimates of national income, consumption, savings, capital formation, accounts of the public sector and consolidated accounts of the nation.

National income is a macroeconomic variable. It is a flow concept measured over a period of time. The meaning of national income is complicated and multi-dimensional. Broadly speaking, national income is the aggregate of money values of goods and services produced in a country during a specified period of time (one year).

Production flow in a country during a specified period consists of a number of heterogeneous commodities and services. These include motor cars, wheat, sugar, tea, services of doctors and teachers and thousands of such other items. These diverse items having their own distinct physical features and units of measurement cannot be added together. If we wish to total them up in a meaningful manner, it is necessary to give them a common expression, i.e. to use some kind of common unit. Money is the unit used for this purpose. Every product and service has a money value in the market (price) and by adding up money values of different goods and services we get a total called national income.

Importance of National Income Statistics: National income statistics serve a number of useful purposes.

1. With the help of a time-series data of national income of a country, we can review the economic performance of that country, i.e. whether its economy is progressing or declining. If it is progressing then at what rate? Similarly, fluctuations in national income over a period of time reveal the degree of stability or instability prevailing in an economy.

2. National income estimates give details of the composition of national income, i.e. the industry of origin. Changes in the relative shares of agriculture, industry and service sector in national income indicate structural changes in the pattern of production. An increase in the share of industry generally means growing modernisation, urbanisation and specialisation in the economy.

3. National income statistics provide useful information regarding its distribution among various factors of production, and also among various decile groups of population. The distribution of national income provides information regarding the degree of economic inequalities and changes thereof. This information is important for evaluating egalitarian policies of the government. The

distribution of national income by factor shares measures the changes in the share of labour and capital and therefore reflects the variations in the productivity of these groups.

4. The utilisation of national income (national expenditure) provides information regarding changes in the share of consumption expenditure and capital formation. Such changes give an idea of the extent by which the capital assets of a country are increasing or decreasing.

5. The usefulness of national income statistics is all the more important in countries where economic planning is a strategy of development process. Economic planners fix targets in terms of percentage increase in national income, and the successful implementation of plans is also assessed with reference to these targets. Desired changes in the distribution of national income may also be an objective of economic planning.

6. Another significance of national income statistics lies in international comparisons. Which countries of the world are prosperous and which are poor can be known by comparing national income statistics, or more appropriately per capita income figures. The economic performance (rate of growth) of one country vis-à-vis other countries is also understood in terms of these statistics.

International comparison of national income is more difficult than the comparison over time because different nations use different monetary units having different purchasing power for estimation of national income. Even the criteria used for the estimation purpose differ, i.e. coverage and methods employed are also different. For purposes of international comparison, various monetary units are converted into US dollar with the help of exchange rates. However, due to fluctuating exchange rates, the comparison is not very accurate. Furthermore, products represented by the national income are often different and satisfy different needs determined by local climatic conditions and institutional factors obtaining in different countries.

In view of the foregoing significance, most modern economies make estimates of national income for use by the policymakers and the general public.

Methods of Measuring National Income: National income of a country can be measured in three different ways: from the angle of production, income generation, and final utilisation (expenditure). These three forms are circular in nature. According to production approach, productive units engage capital and labour and turn out goods and services, the total measure of which gives the national product. This production process generates a given amount of money income which is distributed by the productive units to the factors of production. The measure of income in the manner indicates the share of national product distributed to the factors of production or in other words the national income by factor shares. The income thus received by the factors of production is then spent either by households for consumption purpose or by the producers for acquiring more capital to increase the physical assets of their production units. The national income by definition is the same whether measured at the point of production or at the stage of income generation or at the stage of final utilisation. In other words, the total of net output, income flows, the final expenditure are identical. The significance of each method arises from the fact that they reflect total operations of the economy at the levels of three basic economic functions, viz. production, distribution and disposition.

National income may be measured by any one of the three foregoing approaches. It is difficult to say which method is superior to the other because the applicability of a particular method depends upon the availability of data in a country and also the purpose of national income estimates.

Ideally, national income should be estimated by all the three methods for purposes of cross-checking, and also for a complete analysis of the economy. By comparing the results obtained by different methods, the estimating agency can find out the discrepancies and make suitable adjustments for arriving at the final figure. Moreover, the details of the three different methods provide useful information regarding various aspects of the economic progress.

Various Concepts of National Income: National income is a multi-faceted concept. A number of estimates are used having totals which are more inclusive than others. This is so because there is disagreement among economists over what to include and what to exclude as national income. The other reason for the variety of estimates is that certain estimates may be more useful for one purpose, and a different estimate for another purpose. The basic concepts and definitions of the terms used in national accounts are as follows:

National Versus Domestic Concept: In a closed economy people consume goods and services produced within its borders. National and domestic product/income are synonymous for such an economy. However, most countries of the world are open economies having trade and financial relations with other countries of the world. Thus, a part of total production in India is exported to foreign countries and a variety of goods are imported into India from other countries. Similarly, people in India have made investments abroad on which they receive payments of interest or dividends from foreigners. Likewise, foreigners have made investments in our country on which we make payments. Also, we give to and receive from other countries gifts and grants for various purposes. If we take into account all these items, viz. exports and imports, gifts, loans, factor income flows, we measure national product/income.

Domestic product/income is that product/income which arises out of the activities of economic agents within the country even if a part of that income accrues to non-residents. When adjustments are made to this product by deducting the incomes of non-residents within the country and adding the income of residents abroad, the national product/income is obtained. The difference between the national and domestic concepts is the net factor income from abroad.

Gross Versus Net Value Added: Capital is one of the primary factors used in the production process. During the course of production, a part of physical capital (machinery and buildings etc.) is worn out, i.e. its economic life is reduced. If depreciated capital is not replaced, the production in the country will gradually decline in the years to come. If we want to sustain the present level of national income, we must deduct from gross output the depreciation of capital during the reference period. What is left after the deduction is net national product which the country can consume and still maintain the present level of output. Ordinarily, a country will consume less than its net national income and use the surplus to increase its capital stock for increasing output in the future.

National product/income can be measured either on a gross basis or on a net basis. Net national product is simply gross national product less the estimated amount of depreciation (i.e. consumption of fixed capital) during the year.

Factor Cost Versus Market Prices: The value of goods and services produced in a country are ordinarily measured at prices at which these are traded in the market. When we buy a tube of toothpaste the price we pay includes an element of tax like excise duty or sales tax (indirect taxes). Thus, the payment we make does not go wholly to the people who produce the goods. A part of the payment goes to the government in the form of taxes. This payment to government does not reflect the true cost of producing the goods concerned. Contrarily, when the government pays subsidies (say to handloom weavers) the money incomes of factors exceed the market value of their output. Valuation of goods at market prices violates the basic principle that the value of goods produced is equal to the sum of the money income received by the factors of production. Similarly, the various forms of final output when considered from the point of expenditure valued at market prices will exceed the total obtained at factor cost by the amount of indirect taxes reduced by the value of subsidies. In order to get a total of national income which corresponds to the income payments actually received by factors of production, we must subtract the total of indirect taxes from and add the value of subsidies to national income measured at market prices. Hence,

National income at factor cost = National income at market prices - Indirect taxes + Subsidies

It is noteworthy that not all types of taxes add to the prices of commodities sold in the market. For example, personal income tax (a direct tax) is levied after the factor shares are received. Since such a tax is not levied during the course of production, it does not add to the prices of goods. It is the taxes on commodities (customs, excises, and sales taxes) which add to the prices of goods.

Current Versus Constant Prices: National income may be measured both at current and constant prices. At current prices it shows the total income during a year in terms of the prices prevailing in that particular year. For purposes of comparison over years it is not a true measure of real income because a part of the increase may be due to rising prices. For example, if we want to compare real national income during 1999-2000 with that during 1980-81 (base year) we must make adjustment for the price rise during the intervening period. For this purpose we multiply the production of 1999-2000 with the prices prevailing in 1980-81. The adjustment figures for 1999-2000 would now be strictly comparable with 1980-81, because they reflect greater or lesser output of goods and services. When national income of a particular year is measured in terms of the price level of some base year (1980-81), it is measured at constant prices or in real terms. In other words, it is stated in terms of 1980-81 rupees considering the foregoing example. The national income in real terms provides a measure of the growth of the economy. The formula for converting national income at current prices to income at constant prices is as follows:

National income at current prices X 100 / Index of current prices = National income at constant prices

National Income and Economic Progress: Can increase in national income be considered an index of economic progress? The relationship between national income and economic progress is subject to certain qualifications. An increase in national income at current prices does not necessarily mean economic progress because such an increase may be due to rising prices. Therefore, the first condition is that increase in national income should be real, i.e. in terms of constant prices.

Even if national income increases in real terms it cannot be said to lead to economic progress necessarily. A better index of economic progress is increase in per capita income. For this purpose we have to consider the population variable. Clearly, if real national income and population increase at the same rate, the per capita real income will remain the same. For the per capita real income to increase, it is necessary that the rate of increase in real national income is more than proportionate to the rate of increase in population. Since economic progress means increase in real per capita income, it can happen when the following two conditions are satisfied: (a) there is increase in real national income and (b) the rate of increase in real national income is more than the rate of increase in population.

National Income and Economic Welfare: Does an increase in national income necessarily mean increase in economic welfare of the people? The answer to this question is subject to various qualifications.

National income is a measure of the value of goods and services produced in a year. These goods and services satisfy the wants of the people and therefore it is generally believed that the national income is reflective of the satisfaction or economic welfare of the people. In other words, the higher the national income, the greater the economic well-being of the people. However, the validity of this statement is subject to a number of adjustments.

It is well known that the estimates of national income do not include, due to technical reasons, certain goods and services which increase satisfaction of the people. For example, the services of housewives to the family members are excluded from national income calculations. Similarly, the satisfaction which people derive from leisure does not form part of national income. Satisfaction derived from leisure and from the services of family members ought to be included in national income in order to get a true measure of economic welfare.

Conversely, certain deductions ought to be made from the usual concept of national income. The modern production process involves pollution of the environment (air, water, and calmness) which reduces welfare of the people. Moreover, certain expenditures of the government are wasteful and therefore do not add to economic welfare. Expenditure on defence, control of riots etc. though necessary, are unproductive. They are sometimes called *regrettable costs*. These items ought to be deducted from national income in order to arrive at a true measure of economic welfare. In brief,

Net economic welfare = National income + Value of leisure + Services of family members - Environment pollution - Regrettable costs.

The composition of national income is another determinant of economic welfare. If a great deal of production consists of war goods or other injurious items like cigarettes and liquor, the national income figures will not truly reflect economic welfare. However, instead of tanks and missiles if a greater part of national income is composed of textiles, sugar, milk and other wage goods, it will indicate enhanced economic well-being of the people.

Economic welfare also depends on the manner in which national income is distributed among the people. Highly unequal distribution may increase the welfare of a small section of the population while the majority of the people remain deprived. It is therefore necessary to find out the degree of inequality in income distribution before drawing conclusion from national income figures.

In short, national income in its usual meaning is not necessarily an index of economic welfare of the people. The estimates of national income ought to be modified in terms of foregoing adjustments in order to be reflective of economic well-being.

Difficulties in Calculating National Income: Many intricate problems arise in the practical work of computing national income. Some of these problems are conceptual in nature while others pertain to accuracy of computation, e.g. avoiding double counting.

There are definitional problems concerning the very concept of national income, i.e. what to include and exclude as national income. For example, should we include household production in national income or not. It is true that we purchase most of the goods and services in the market. Still, many productive activities take place in our homes. Housewives cook food, stitch clothes and help the school-going children to do homework. Men of the household occasionally repair furniture and grow fruit and vegetables in the kitchen garden. All these activities constitute production. Similarly, most houses are owned by the occupants and therefore no rent is paid for them. These are some of the examples which should form part of the stream of the goods and services which make up the national income. If we include in national income goods and services traded in the market and exclude similar goods and services produced at home, it would be illogical. Although we wish to include household production in national income, it is not always possible to do so. In some cases it is possible because the facility has a market equivalent. For example, we can find and include in national income the rental value of owner-occupied houses. However, much of the work done in home has no market equivalent. What is the monetary worth of nursing services of a mother for her sick child? It is indeed difficult to say. In view of these difficulties, the economist has to make a compromise and exclude the services of housewives from national income.

Limitations of National Income Statistics: National income estimates are not measures of human satisfaction. These estimates take into account goods and services which are traded in the market, and leave out, due to measurement problems, various productive and useful activities which go in our homes. There are also technical difficulties which reduce accuracy of these estimates.

In spite of the various limitations and problems in their measurement, national income statistics are not only important but indispensable for planners and policymakers.

National Wealth and National Capital

United Nations Statistical Office (UNSO) has defined national wealth as "total of various kinds of net tangible and intangible non-financial assets of residents, plus financial claims on non-residents less financial liabilities to non-residents". Tangible assets are further classified into (a) reproducible tangible assets (machines etc.) and (b) non-reproducible tangible assets (land, minerals).

National capital of a country is that part of national wealth which is reproducible. More specifically, national capital stock refers to reproducible tangible assets. It consists of all resources which contribute to the production of goods and services. Reproducible tangible assets comprise: (a) fixed assets and (b) stocks (i.e. inventories). The reproducible fixed assets, commonly known as fixed capital stock, consists of: (i) residential and non-residential buildings, (ii) dams, irrigation and flood control projects, (iii) transport equipment, (iv) machinery and plants, (v) breading stock, (vi) expenditure on land improvement, plantations and orchard development. The stocks include inventories of goods producing industries, trade and stocks of government services.

The following assets do not form part of capital stock: (a) durable goods in the hands of households which are not used for further production of goods and services do not form part of fixed capital stock as, for example, automobiles, refrigerators, washing machines, furniture and sewing machines, (b) fixed assets mainly meant for defence purposes do not form part of capital stock such as warships, fighter aircrafts, transport vehicles, and war materials.

Reliable estimates of capital stock of a country are helpful in projecting future production possibilities of the economy. These estimates also provide the basis for estimating capital consumption needed to compute various macroeconomic aggregates on net basis.

Estimation of national capital stock is no easy task. The most formidable difficulty is the problem of annual valuation of various types of assets included in the definition of capital stock. Annual valuation may be ascertained on the basis of market value or the earning capacity. The second serious problem pertains to the assessment of depreciation. There is hardly any scientific approach to this problem. Estimation of national capital is a serious problem in underdeveloped countries like India where adequate and reliable statistics are not available. Serious difficulties are encountered with regard to valuation of stock in unorganised sector.

Negative Correlation **See Correlation**

Negative Income Tax

The term negative income tax, attributed to Milton Friedman, means assessing subsidy benefit on an income base. It provides for entitlement for a beneficiary unit on the basis of negative deviation of income from some *break even* income level. Income tax assesses liability on positive deviation of income from *break even* level.

Neo-Cambridge Approach to Balance of Payments **See Balance of Payments**

Neo-colonialism **See Economic Imperialism**

Neo-mercantilism **See Economic Imperialism**

Net Accretion Theory of Income

It defines income as net accretion to economic power between two periods of time. This comprehensive definition of income for tax purposes takes into account the following forms of income: (a) cash income, e.g. wages, dividends and interest received, (b) accrued income like interest credited (instead of paid), appreciation in the value of assets (capital gains) which continue to be held, (c) imputed income, such as imputed rent from owner-occupied residence or fringe benefits (like subsidised or free accommodation available to company executives), (d) transfer incomes which are received by taxpayers from other parties including the government. Pensions and alimony payments are good examples of transfer incomes. Although transfer incomes are not included in national income, they are part of the net accretion theory. An equitable tax system should include all forms of income stated above in the tax base.

Theoretically, it is possible to define income comprehensively. However, practical difficulties arise in measuring many of the elements included in the above definition. Various forms of imputed and accrued incomes pose serious measurement problems.

1. Income received in kind poses serious difficulties. When remuneration for services of a factor is paid in kind rather than in cash, evaluation problems arise. For example, free meals and transport facilities provided by the employer add to the real income of the employees and hence form part of the net accretion theory. Such benefits are elements of indirect wages. If benefits in kind are not subject to taxation, it would encourage employers to pass on remuneration to their employees in large doses of income-in-kind rather than cash payment. The employees can reduce or even avoid their tax liability through these means.

Hence, tax laws of most countries take into account perquisites and fringe benefits while determining the tax base. Should benefits received in kind be evaluated at their cost to the employer or in terms of the benefit accruing to the employees? Should all types of benefits-in-kind be included in the taxable base? These are questions without clear-cut answers. For example, the income tax law of India includes perquisites like rent-free accommodation in the definition of salary but exempts from tax, perquisites in the form of medical facilities provided by the employer.

2. Another difficulty relates to Imputed Income (q.v.) which arises when a taxpayer is himself the producer and the consumer of a given commodity or service.

3. Several problems arise in computing accrued incomes for tax purpose. For example, how to treat the accrual of income in the form of a share in the undistributed profits of a company.

4. Capital gains are a part of taxable income according to the net accretion theory. However, it does not distinguish between realised and unrealised capital gains. While most income tax systems include realised capital gains in the tax base, none perhaps does so as regards unrealised capital gains. Since physical assets of business and household are not traded continually, it is difficult to compute their market value from year to year for the purpose of calculating capital gains. Likewise, financial assets (like unquoted shares) pose problems of valuation.

5. Yet another limitation of the net accretion principle is its failure to distinguish between nominal and real income. Income is considered as an appropriate measure of an individual's ability-to-pay. Should this ability be viewed in nominal or real terms? If in real terms, then it requires indexation of income.

In view of the limitations mentioned above, the net accretion principle is far from being fully implemented by any income tax system in the world. The actual income tax system deviates, in varying degrees, from this definition due to administrative and policy considerations.

It is indeed very difficult to reduce the concept of income to a precise and unambiguous definition. In practice, guidance is sought from judicial pronouncements on the subject. Income tax laws of different countries normally exemplify rather than define income. See also Source Theory of Income.

Net Barter Terms of Trade See Terms of Trade

Net Factor Income from Abroad

Non-resident workers work in the domestic territory of some other country and earn wages and salaries. Similarly, people can acquire property (like factories, shops and buildings) and financial assets (bonds and shares) abroad. The sum total of wages, rent, interest and profit is the income earned from abroad for their country and for themselves.

Net factor income from abroad is the difference between the income received from abroad for rendering factor services and the income paid for the factor services rendered by non-residents in the domestic territory of a country.

Net Value Added at Factor Cost See Value of Output

Net Value Added at Market Prices See Value of Output

Net Worth

It is the value of a business attributable to the ordinary shareholders. This value comprises the total assets of the business less liabilities to all those other than ordinary shareholders.

Neutrality in Taxation

Relative prices determined by competitive market forces tend to ensure the most efficient allocation of resources in an economy. Taxes cause distortions in relative prices and therefore reduce productive efficiency. According to the neutrality rule, taxes should not interfere with consumers' choices and if they do, it would entail a sub-optimal allocation of resources.

However, arguments in favour of neutrality are abstract and based on rather unrealistic assumptions, e.g. perfectly competitive markets. It is difficult to devise a fiscal system which exerts no influence on the economic behaviour of consumers and producers.

The spirit of neutrality principle requires least interference by taxes in the working of a competitive market. For example, a sales tax on the generality of goods will cause lesser distortion than excise duty on a few specified commodities.

New International Economic Order (NIEO)

It was adopted as a resolution at the Sixth Special Session of the UN General Assembly. A call was given by developing countries for revolutionary changes in international economic system, for improving trade relations, expanding exports and stabilising their real earnings and increasing the exports of manufactured goods in place of primary products alone. It further called for more aid, debt relief and trade concessions to LDCs.

Nominal Exchange Rate **See Exchange Rate**

Nominal Rate of Tax

Rate of tax approved by the legislature is termed as nominal (or statutory) rate. It can be misleading when one takes into account exclusions, deductions, allowances, tax credits and tax evasion. These erosions in the tax base considerably reduce the Average Tax Rate (q.v.) below the statutory one.

Non-antagonistic Mode of Production **See Mode of Production**

Non-banking Financial Companies (NBFCs)

These are financial intermediaries which provide a variety of services including equipment leasing, hire purchase, loans, investments and chit fund activities. This sector comprises a heterogeneous lot of privately-owned, small-sized financial intermediaries.

Non-competing Groups

It is a term used in labour economics to mean groups of workers which do not compete with each other for employment. Non-compering groups arise when certain jobs require extraordinary skills possessed by a relatively small number of persons. Thus, fighter pilots and heart surgeons do not compete with unskilled workers and hence belong to non-competing groups. Conversely, unskilled workers and semi-skilled workers compete with each other for a variety of jobs like that of a peon, watchman, delivery boy and shop assistant.

Non-durable Goods **See Durable Goods and Non-durable Goods**

Non-linear (curvilinear) Correlation **See Correlation**

Non-recurring Income **See Casual Income**

Non-tariff Barriers

They refer to a long list of quantitative restrictions like quotas, import-licensing, prohibition and embargo, performance standards, dumping regulations and customs valuation procedures which governments impose on imports to achieve its trade policy goals.

Normative Economics **See Positive Economics and Normative Economics**

North-South Dialogue

It is a term used for mutual exchange of ideas on economic and social issues between the rich and the developing countries.

NOSTRO Account

Account of a bank in a foreign bank is called nostro account. For example, a London bank's dollar account in a New York bank is a nostro account.

Nuisance Variables

These are factors which adversely affect LDCs by raising their import dependence, curbing their savings and distorting their distribution of income. International demonstration effect is one such nuisance variable which encourages conspicuous consumption by affecting tastes and habits.

O

Octroi

It is a tax on the entry of goods into a local area from other areas for the purpose of consumption or sale. Though an important source of revenue for local bodies, it obstructs the free movement of vehicles carrying goods across the country. Octroi was completely abandoned in France in 1949.

Offer Curve

Offer curve (also called reciprocal demand curve) is a locus of all the points showing different quantities of a commodity which a country is willing and offering to exchange for another commodity. Given two countries A and B, it refers to A's demand for B's products and B's demand for A's products. It is the relative intensity of this reciprocal demand for each other which determines the terms of trade. This is generally shown with the help of offer curves. Offer curve analysis is based on the principle of reciprocal demand which was formulated in 1848 by classical economist John Stuart Mill (1806-1873). Offer curves as such were developed by F.Y. Edgeworth (1845-1926) and Alfred Marshall (1842-1924) to show the determination of terms of trade.

Official Rate

It is that rate of exchange which is approved and maintained by the government and at which official transactions and movements of currency take place.

Oil Facility

It was started by International Monetary Fund (IMF) in 1974-75 in response to urgent need of member countries to finance increased deficits resulting from the spurt in import cost of petroleum and its products. To finance these drawings under oil facility, IMF borrowed funds from oil exporting countries and other countries having stable balance of payments position.

Oligopoly

It is a market structure characterised by few sellers and many buyers. An oligopoly is an industry comprising only a few competing firms. These firms are strong rivals constantly watching jealously each other's decisions and reacting accordingly. This type of market structure is frequently observed in real life as, for example, car manufacturers.

An oligopolistic market may emerge because of falling costs due to the economies of large-scale production. In some cases, an industry may be dominated by a few large firms because they are successful in preventing the entry of new firms.

Price Stickiness and the Kinked Demand Curve: If we assume oligopoly with product differentiation, then it is possible for a producer to raise his price without fearing to lose all his customers. In other words, his demand curve is negatively sloped. This type of market situation has a strange phenomenon called *price stickiness* or *price rigidity*. It means firms in oligopoly prefer to keep prices unchanged unless there are violent fluctuations in demand or cost conditions. The explanation for sticky prices lies in the possible reactions of competitor firms. These reactions are of such a nature that they give rise to an unusual type of demand curve of an oligopolist firm. This unusual demand curve (or average revenue curve) is called the *kinked demand curve*, as shown in the Figure below. It is clear that there is no revenue function for an oligopolistic firm.

Let us assume that the price is settled down at OP and all firms are selling the product at this price. The firm in question is selling OM of its own product. Now if this firm raises its price, it is believed that none of the competitors will follow suit. A modest increase in the price of the firm's product will lead to a very large fall in its sales. In other words, demand is very elastic if one firm alone raises its price. Conversely, if the firm cuts its price, all the rival firms cut their prices to exactly the same extent. It means the demand is inelastic if all firms cut their prices. These possible reactions of rival firms discourage the firm in question from deviating from the existing position. Technically speaking, the firm is faced with a demand curve YXZ which has a kink at point X.

The Figure shows also the shape of the marginal revenue (MR) curve associated with the kinked demand curve. Portion AB is the section of the MR curve associated with YX portion of the composite demand curve. Similarly, CD is associated with XZ. There is a *gap* or *hole* (BC) in the MR curve. This is due to the fact that MR curve associated with YX and XZ portions of the demand curve has different slopes and positions.

Equilibrium of an Oligopolist Firm: In the Figure, the MR curve is shown with a gap between points B and C. If the MC curve passes through the *gap* (as depicted in the figure) the firm has no reason to change the price. It means the firm will not change price so long as the MC curve passes through any point between B and C. However, if MC curve rises sufficiently to pass through AB portion of MR curve, the firm will consider raising the price. Conversely, if the MC curve falls sufficiently to pass through CD portion of MR curve, the firm will consider lowering the price.

Thus, economic analysis suggests a general tendency for oligopolistic prices to be sticky unless there are significant changes in cost or demand conditions.

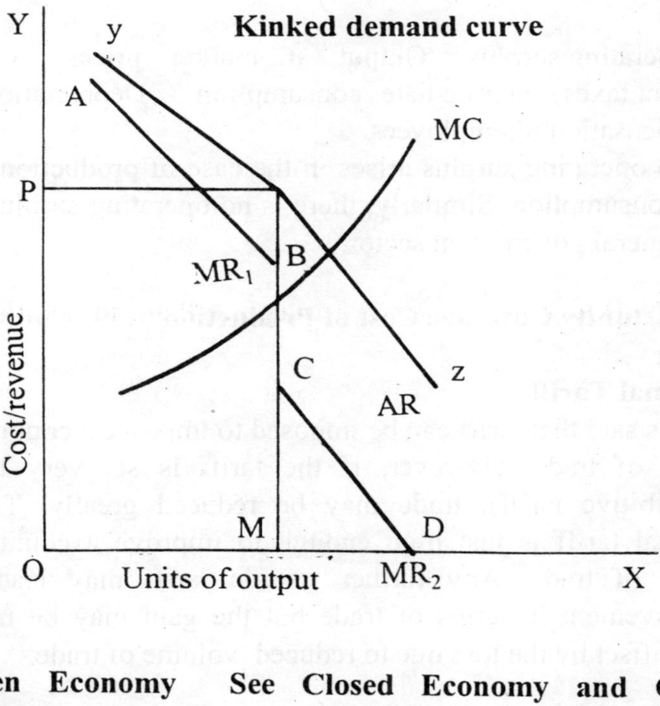

Open Economy **See Closed Economy and Open Economy**

Open Market Operations **See Central Bank**

Operating Surplus

Operating surplus is the sum of property income and income from entrepreneurship. Property income consists of interest, rent on land and buildings (rents actually received as well as imputed rent of owner-occupied buildings), royalties for the use of mineral deposits, patents and copyrights and trade marks. Income from entrepreneurship is the second component of operating surplus. It consists of profit for organising production and undertaking attendant risks.

Operating surplus = Output at market prices - Net indirect taxes - Intermediate consumption - Depreciation - Compensation of employees.

No operating surplus arises in the case of production for self-consumption. Similarly, there is no operating surplus in the general government sector.

Opportunity Cost See Cost of Production

Optimal Tariff

It is said that tariff can be imposed to improve a country's terms of trade. However, if the tariff is set very high (prohibitive tariff), trade may be reduced greatly. Thus, optimal tariff is just high enough to improve a country's terms of trade. Any further rise in tariff may lead to improvement in terms of trade but the gain may be more than offset by the loss due to reduced volume of trade.

Optimal Taxation

It advocates a system of taxation which generates the least loss of welfare. Optimal taxation involves a variety of questions like the ratio between direct and indirect taxes, progressivity of taxes, trade off between equity and efficiency and other related issues.

Organisation for Economic Co-operation and Development (OECD)

It is an international organisation of industrialised nations with the following twofold objectives: 1. To contribute through co-operative efforts to economic growth, employment, financial stability and rising standard of living in member countries. 2. To promote economic development of all nations and trade among them by assisting countries in their efforts to achieve these goals.

Based in Paris, OECD was formed on December 14, 1960 as a successor organisation to the Organisation for European Economic Co-operation (OEEC), whose main purpose was to co-ordinate the post-World War II economic recovery of Europe and to administer aid provided by USA through the Marshall Plan. In addition to the 18 European members of the OEEC, USA and Canada were among the original member countries. Since then, Australia, Finland, Japan and New Zealand have joined the organisation.

There are numerous committees and semiautonomous agencies that carry on the work of OECD. An indication of the multitude of topics covered by the OECD is given by the various committees which cover economic policy, energy, development assistance, technical co-operation, trade, international investment, multinational enterprises, insurance, financial markets, consumer affairs, tourism, sea transport, work force, education, environment, science, industry, agriculture and other areas of concern. Many of these committees have further subcommittees or working parties.

The following semiautonomous agencies operate within the OECD framework: International Energy Agency created in 1974 to assist in the implementation of energy policies; Nuclear Energy Agency which was established in 1958 to promote the use of nuclear power for peaceful purposes; Development Centre, which has responsibilities in areas of research, liaison, information exchange and expert assistance related to development problems; Road Research Programme; Educational Research and Innovation Centre; and Interfutures Project, which is a long-range study and analysis group.

Among the wide variety of functions and tasks performed by the OECD are the collection and dissemination of statistical information on the member countries and conduct of basic research and policy studies. The Secretariat maintains extensive data bank and publishes relevant statistical information on the member countries. It also engages in regular economic forecasting exercises and publishes their findings. On a more formal level, the OECD Council may adopt decisions which are binding upon member countries or recommendations for their voluntary consideration and possible implementation.

Outside Currency **See Currency**

Overall Budget Deficit

This conventional measure of budgetary deficit refers to the excess of total expenditure (both revenue and capital) over total receipts (both revenue and capital). In other words, it shows the gap in the total receipts and total disbursements of a government. This gap is financed by (a) borrowings from the central bank and (b) draw down of cash balances of a government. This is the conventionally defined budgetary deficit. It is this deficit which determines the growth of liquidity and inflationary pressure in the economy.

Overall budget deficit = Total receipts - Total expenditure.

Overhead Cost **See Fixed Cost**

P

Pacific Economic Co-operation Council (PECC)

PECC is a tripartite, non-governmental organisation committed to promoting economic co-operation in the Pacific Rim. It comprises representatives from 23 Asia-Pacific economies who meet regularly to work on practical government and business policy issues to increase trade, investment and economic development in the region.

It is the only organisation in the region that brings business, government and researchers together on an equal footing to address key trade and investment issues. Though it has an independent agenda, PECC maintains direct links with governments in the region to enable its work to be channelled through Ministers and policymakers.

PECC anticipates emerging economic opportunities and problems for business and governments. In addition, it establishes task groups to address issues in individual sectors on a regional level as well as at the level of individual member economies. It has become a clearing house for policy and business research, serving as a catalyst for new initiatives in policy change.

PECC was formed in 1980 at the initiative of the Prime Ministers of Japan and Australia. They called for the establishment of an independent, regional mechanism to advance economic co-operation and market-driven integration. A vital characteristic of the new body, they asserted, should be its independent, unofficial status which would permit it to address economic issues and measures free of the constraints of formal governmental policies and relationships.

Pareto Optimality **See Welfare Economics**

Partial Correlation **See Correlation**

Partial Equilibrium and General Equilibrium

Partial equilibrium analysis deals with decisions in a particular segment of the economy in isolation of what happens in other segments. It is based on the *ceteris paribus* (other things being equal) assumption. For example, we may study the production decision of a firm on the assumption that factor prices, the state of technology and commodity prices are given. The *ceteris paribus* assumption allows us to study the cost-minimisation behaviour of a firm in isolation from the influence of other factors.

However, any real world economic system is characterised by interdependence among its various segments. Markets of all commodities and all productive factors are inter-related and prices in all markets are simultaneously determined. *A general equilibrium approach is defined as a position in which all markets and all decision-making units are in simultaneous equilibrium.* A general equilibrium exists if each market is cleared at a positive price, with each consumer maximising satisfaction and each firm maximising profit. How this position can be reached is the subject matter of general equilibrium analysis.

General equilibrium emerges from the solution of a simultaneous equation model of millions of equations in millions of unknown. In principle, a simultaneous equation system has a solution if the number of independent equations is equal to the number of unknowns in the system. This approach was followed by the French economist Leon Walras (1834-1910), the founder of general equilibrium analysis.

He argued that all prices and quantities in all markets are determined simultaneously through their interaction with one another. Walras used a system of simultaneous equations to describe the interaction of individual sellers and buyers in all the markets. In the Walrasian model, the behaviour of each individual decision-maker is presented by a set of equations. For example, each consumer has a double role: he buys commodities and sells services of factors to firms. In a general equilibrium system of the Walrasian type there are as many markets as there are commodities and factors of production.

Par Value **See Face Value**

Pay-As-You-Earn (PAYE)

A system of collecting income tax from employees recommended by J.M. Keynes and introduced in Britain in 1944. See also Withholding Tax.

Payroll Tax

It is a tax levied on the payroll of a firm. Paid by the employer, it is based on the amount of wages and salaries paid by him. Payroll tax, essentially a post-World War II phenomenon, is primarily meant to finance schemes which benefit workers. In USA, the Federal Government levies payroll tax on employers to finance the employers' part of the social security programme.

Peacock-Wiseman Hypothesis

In their study of public expenditure trends in the British economy for the period 1890-1955, Alan T. Peacock and Jack Wiseman confirmed the operation of Wagner's Law (q.v.) but they provided a rather complicated and controversial explanation for it.

Behaving like private individuals, governments spend more as they get more. There is automatic increase in tax yield due to enlargement of the tax base in the wake of economic development. The pressure for new spending is always there and if revenues are available the government will seldom hesitate to spend them. It might become cautious if financing of new spending requires raising of tax rates or imposition of new taxes.

Displacement Effect: Apart from this natural growth of expenditure in line with revenues, occasions may arise to finance a war. New taxes are imposed and rates of existing taxes are revised. It has been observed that the tax system does not return to its pre-war position after the war is over. With tax arrangements made during a war being continued after the war, the growth trend of revenues and expenditures is moved upward permanently. Peacock and Wiseman called this movement the d*isplacement effect*.

The displacement hypothesis states that government spending grows over time not at a constant rate but rather stepwise. The movement from one step to another generally coincides with a war. Such disturbances create a displacement effect, shifting public revenues and expenditures to new plateau.

Inspection Effect: There are two aspects of the displacement effect. Firstly, in times of crisis, people accept methods of raising revenues formerly thought intolerable.

The acceptance of new tax levels remains when the disturbance has disappeared. *It is harder to get the saddle on the horse than to keep it there.*

Secondly, social upheavals impose new and continuing responsibilities on governments such as payment of war pensions, reparation payments, rehabilitation of war victims etc. Wars often force the attention of government and people to problems of which they were formerly less conscious. There is, thus, what Peacock and Wiseman call an *inspection effect*. Their hypothesis is not limited to wars but includes the effects of other social upheavals like depressions.

Per Capita Income

Per capita income is a simple but very useful concept in economics. It is calculated by dividing national income by total population of a country.

Per capita income = National income / Population

Increase in real per capita income is the definition of a progressive economy. It is an index of the living standard of the people in a country.

Perfect Competition

Perfect competition is a market situation with the following features:

1. A Perfectly competitive market has a large number of buyers and sellers so that no individual buyer or seller can influence the market price. A firm is a price-taker, i.e. it must accept the price ruling in the market. Since price is given, neither marginal revenue nor average revenue varies with output, and both are equal to price. Technically speaking, the marginal and average revenue curves are the same and parallel to the horizontal axis.

2. All the firms in a competitive market sell homogeneous product. Thus, if a firm tries to charge more than the prevailing market price, it will lose all buyers. There is apparently no reason for the firm to charge less when it can sell any quantity at the going price.

3. Firms enjoy freedom of entry into and freedom of exit from the industry. In other words, existing firms cannot bar the entry of new firms and there are no legal restrictions on entry or exit.

4. Buyers and sellers are well informed about market conditions. For example, a buyer knows when one firm is asking a higher price than other firms.

Peril Point

A tariff reduction may encourage imports in an economy to such a level that the domestic competing industry is imperilled or endangered. An *escape clause* or *peril-point provision* is to be kept in trade policy so as to prevent such an injury. Such a clause or point is made in Reciprocal Trade Agreements (q.v.) so that tariff reduction cannot go beyond a point. This gives an advantage to the domestic business group regardless of its performance on cost or efficiency front.

Periphery and Centre

This concept refers to poor and rich economies respectively. Centre is technologically advanced, has higher income level and standard of living, produces modern and technically superior goods with a high demand elasticity in overseas market. Wage rate is high, labour union are strong and the overall market is monopolistic.

In periphery, low and constant wage rate prevails due to surplus labour force. Also, low productivity, inferior technology, high cost of production, exports of primary products and a high income elasticity of demand are some of the features of the poor countries of the South.

Permanent Income Hypothesis See Consumption Function

Perpetuities See Bond

Perquisite

It means any casual emolument or benefit attached to an office or position in addition to salary or wages. It does not cover mere reimbursement of necessary disbursements. Perquisites may be provided in cash or in kind.

Personal Disposable Income See Private Income and Personal Income

Personal Income See Private Income and Personal Income

Phillips Curve

It is a device used by economists to examine the relationship between inflation and unemployment. The downward sloping Phillips curve shows that over the years a particular rate of unemployment would be accompanied by a particular rate of inflation.

In his 1958 study based on data for UK for the period 1861 to 1957, A.W. Phillips found a long-run stable relationship between the rate of unemployment and the rate at which wage rates increase. A stable relationship between unemployment rate and wage rates implies a stable relationship between the rate of unemployment and the rate of inflation. It shows that a decline in the unemployment rate is accompanied by a rise in the rate of inflation.

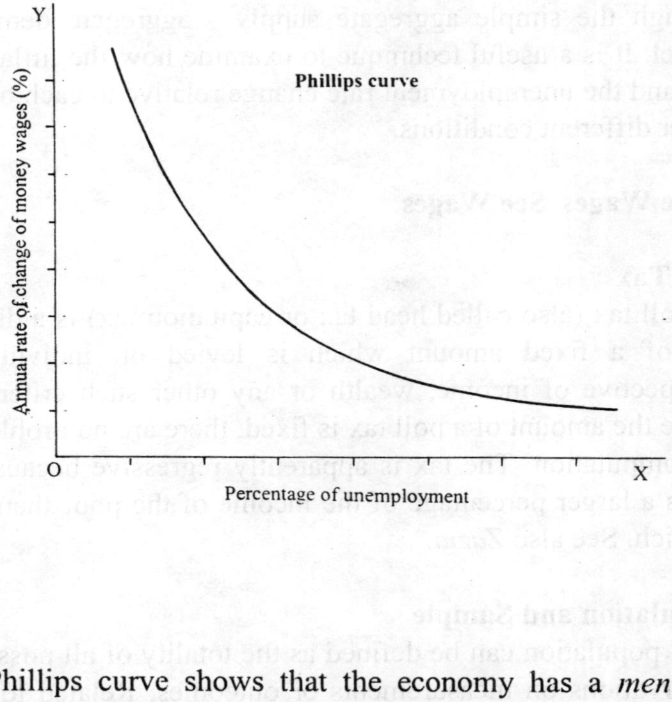

Phillips curve shows that the economy has a *menu of choices* between inflation and unemployment. In other words, there is a trade off in the sense that the economy can achieve a lower rate of unemployment by accepting a higher rate of inflation or it can achieve a lower rate of inflation by accepting a higher rate of unemployment. What the choice should be is a matter of controversy among economists. Does the benefit of a lower unemployment rate exceed the cost of a higher inflation rate or does the benefit of a lower inflation rate exceed the cost of higher unemployment rate? The difficulties of measuring the costs and benefits of specific changes in the inflation rate and the unemployment rate are indeed complex.

Phillips curve enables us to see things that cannot be seen through the simple aggregate supply - aggregate demand model. It is a useful technique to examine how the inflation rate and the unemployment rate change relative to each other under different conditions.

Piece Wages See Wages

Poll Tax

Poll tax (also called head tax or capitation tax) is a direct tax of a fixed amount which is levied on individuals irrespective of income, wealth or any other such criterion. Since the amount of a poll tax is fixed, there are no problems of computation. The tax is apparently regressive because it takes a larger percentage of the income of the poor than of the rich. See also *Zazia*.

Population and Sample

A population can be defined as the totality of all possible observations on measurements or outcomes. Related to the concept of a population is the concept of a sample which is a set of measurements or outcomes selected from the population.

In collecting data concerning characteristics of a group of individuals or objects it is often impossible or impracticable to observe the entire group as, for example, paddy yield in different fields in a region. Thus, instead of examining the entire group, called the *population* or *universe*, researchers examine a small part of the group called sample. If a sample is representative of a population, important conclusions about the population can be inferred from analysis of the sample.

Population Explosion See Demograhic Transition, Theory of

Portfolio

It refers to the list of investments in shares, debentures, bonds etc. that a person or an institution has made.

Portfolio Investment

It refers to investment in bonds and other debt instruments that do not imply ownership. It gives the investor a claim to a fixed return on investment, e.g. a bond bearing a specific rate of interest.

Positioning

It is a recent term used by transnational corporations (TNCs) for perceiving new positions in new countries/ventures so as to judge their sustainable competitive advantage. Positioning can be of the following types: (a) Access-based Positioning: It refers to a systematic study by a TNC of a country's geography, resource base, market, policy environment etc. (b) Need-based Positioning: It is like serving most or all the needs of a particular group of customers. (c) Variety-based Positioning:

It refers to a TNC producing a subset of a firm's products/services.

Positive Correlation **See Correlation**

Positive Economics and Normative Economics

Economic issues involve both facts and feelings. Therefore, a distinction is made between positive and normative economics. Positive economics deals with existing factual situation, i.e. *what is?* Normative economics relates to value judgement, i.e. *what should be?* What is the rate of income tax at the highest slab of income in India is a subject matter of positive economics while what should be the rate of tax at the highest slab of income falls within the purview of normative economics.

Positive economics is less controversial because facts can be ascertained after careful scrutiny. However, normative economics is complex because opinions of people on economic issues are influenced by differing political, cultural and social beliefs.

Poverty Line

Poverty is a widespread social evil in underdeveloped countries of the world, particularly in Asia and Africa. There is no standard definition of poverty for all the countries of the world. Being a relative concept, the meaning of poverty differs from country to country. In India, poverty is defined in terms of a minimum (subsistence) level of living rather than a reasonable level of living. Thus, minimum physical quantities of cereals, pulses, clothing etc. are determined for a subsistence level. These physical quantities are multiplied by their prices and converted into monetary terms, determining the per capita consumption/income for subsistence level. Persons whose income/consumption is below this determined figure are considered to be below the poverty line.

Hence, poverty line is based on the definition of a norm which takes nutritional requirements into account and all persons below the norm are classified as poor. The present basis of the estimation of poverty line is based on the desired requirements of calories of 2,400 per person per day in the rural areas and 2,100 per person per day in the urban areas. The monetary expenditure per capita needed for meeting these calorie requirements is revised upward periodically taking into consideration the rise in the prices of consumption goods.

Preference Shares

It is a class of shares with a claim on the company's earnings before payment is made on the common shares. Preference shares are normally entitled to dividend at a fixed rate which depends on the terms of the issue. Preference shares are usually entitled to priority if the company is liquidated.

Preferential Duty

It is an import duty levied at a relatively low level so as to favour imports of a particular commodity or imports from a particular country. See also Commonwealth Preference; and Discriminating Duty.

Presumptive Tax

Presumptive tax relates to the use of appropriate indicators of income, wealth etc. instead of the actual records of these tax bases. In the case of income tax, a presumptive tax is imposed on the basis of an estimated taxable income. Presumptive income is exogenously determined. The base for presumptive income tax is fixed and does not depend on the behaviour of individual entrepreneurs. In fact, a presumptive income tax works like a lump sum tax and therefore does not impose marginal tax burden on actual income. Varying methods of presumptive taxation are in operation in Israel, Argentina, Chile, Columbia, and India. The French forfait system is a typical example of presumptive taxation.

The chief advantage of presumptive taxation is its simplicity, both for tax collectors and taxpayers. Thus, it is cost-effective for the administration. Its simplicity encourages tax compliance. Presumptive taxation particularly suits developing countries with a large unorganised business sector consisting of small retail establishments, and self-employed professionals. It is easy to administer this tax which can become an effective source of revenue. In addition, it promotes horizontal equity. See also Forfait Method.

Price-earning Ratio

It is the ratio of the price of a share to its earnings. It is the most widely accepted guide to determine whether or not to buy or sell shares. Firms with good growth rates often earn high profits and hence record a high P/E ratio.

Price Mechanism See Market Mechanism

Price Stickiness See Oligopoly

Primary and Secondary Securities

Primary securities are created by real sector units of the economy (joint stock companies) engaged in the production of goods. Shares and debentures issued by companies are good examples of primary securities.

Secondary securities are created by financial institutions or intermediaries who are not the ultimate borrowers of funds. These institutions raise funds from public to make investments in primary securities. Some examples of secondary securities are bank deposits, units of Unit Trust of India and shares of mutual funds.

Principles of Local Finance **See Local Finance, Principles of**

Principles of Taxation **See Canons of Taxation**

Private Company and Public Limited Company

Private company means a company which (a) restricts the right to transfer its shares, (b) limits the number of its members to fifty and (c) prohibits any invitation to the public to subscribe for any shares in the company. The violation of these conditions will make it a public limited company.

Private Cost **See Cost of Production**

Private Foreign Investment **See Foreign Direct Investment**

Private Income and Personal Income

Private income is derived from national income by adding the sum of government transfer payments and interest on national debt and subtracting the property income of government departments and profits of government enterprises.

Private income = National income - Government transfer payments + Interest on national debt - Property income of government departments - Profits of government enterprises + Net current transfers from abroad.

Personal income is a measure of the actual income receipts of persons from all sources. It is likely that all private income is not paid to the people as money income. It is well known that a part of the earnings of the companies is taken away by the government as corporation tax before being distributed to shareholders. Furthermore, many companies retain a part of the after-tax earnings for making additions to company's plant and machinery or as a reserve for future emergencies. That part of the after-tax earnings which is not distributed among the shareholders is called undistributed profit. In calculating the undistributed profits, allowance is made for increase or decrease in inventories of materials and unsold goods by firms during the year.

Personal income can be derived from private income by subtracting from the latter, corporation tax and undistributed profits of companies.

Personal Income = Private income - Corporation tax - Undistributed profits.

Measurement of personal income is significant as it indicates the ability of the people to pay taxes.

Personal Disposable Income: Personal Disposable income measures how much is actually at the disposal of the people for their consumption or savings. All of the income received by the people does not belong to them. A part of their income is taken away by the government in the form of personal income tax and other compulsory payments to the government (like traffic fines). If we deduct personal taxes from personal income, the remainder is disposable income.

Personal disposable income = Personal income - Personal taxes - Miscellaneous receipts of the government (traffic fines etc.).

Measurement of personal disposable income is significant in various ways. 1. It indicates the purchasing power of consumers. 2. It can be used by business firms as a proxy for potential demand for goods. 3. It can be used by economists to study consumption and saving behaviour in the economy.

Private Placement

The term refers to sale/issue of securities to an institutional investor through direct contact.

Privatisation

The term privatisation conveys a variety of ideas: (a) outright denationalisation, (b) diluting public sector capital holding, (c) allowing private sector in areas hitherto reserved for public sector and (d) general deregulation and liberalisation of industrial and trade activities.

Process-based Division of Labour See Division of Labour

Product-based Division of Labour See Division of Labour

Product Cycle

Highlighted by Raymond Vernon, it refers to a cyclical pattern in technology development. It suggests the following three stage cycle in the life of each product: (a) new product stage, when it has just been launched, (b) maturing product stage, when the product is well set in production and market and (c) standardised product stage, when its technique of production is stabilised.

At stage (a) technology is new and therefore expensive, forming a major part of cost of production. At stage (b) technology is well known and its cost falls with the passage of time; but marketing and capital costs (due to rapid obsolescence of equipment) are the dominant costs. At stage (c) the product is standardised and technology has become stable. The main cost component at this stage is production cost (raw materials, capital and labour).

In terms of determining the comparative advantage and trade pattern, industrial countries will have comparative advantage in the first and second stages. They can export any new commodity since they are technologically advanced and have abundance of capital, managerial and marketing expertise. It is in the third stage only that other countries having raw material, capital and unskilled labour force will start having comparative advantage. It is also known as *flying geese pattern* of development.

Product Differentiation

The concept of product differentiation is used in the theory of monopolistic competition as propounded by E. H. Chamberlin (1899-1967). The theory refers to competition among a large number of firms selling similar but differentiated products. A product (say toothpaste) is differentiated if some significant basis exists for distinguishing the product of one seller from that of another. Such a basis may be real or fancied. Various methods used to distinguish a product from those of the rival firms include different shape, design and packing.

Production

Production is creation of utility. Whosoever creates utility is a producer. One may create utility by transferring a commodity from one place to another. The utility of sand is increased when it is transferred from the river bank to the construction site of a building. Similarly, utility of a commodity may increase if preserved over a period of time. It is generally believed that older the wine the more utility it has. In most cases, utility is created by changing the shape of a commodity. A log of wood has less utility than a table made out of it. Thus, a carpenter who makes the table is a producer. Production includes the following:

1. All the goods and services which are sold in the market with a view to earn profit.

2. Goods and services not sold in the market but which are supplied free or at a nominal price. Most of the government services rendered to the citizens of the country like defence, law and order, public health, street lighting, construction and maintenance of roads, provision of parks are some examples. Services provided by voluntary organisations such as charitable hospitals, schools and colleges are some other examples.

3. Produced goods which fail to reach the market and hence are not sold. This refers to production for own use as, for example, farmers keeping a part of their production for their own consumption. Production for own use is called *own account production*. It includes products of agriculture, livestock, forestry, fishing, mining, cloth weaving etc.

4. Own account production of fixed assets by government, business enterprises, and households. Own account production of fixed assets by government, enterprises and voluntary organisations refers to construction of buildings, roads, machinery and equipment. In the case of households it means agricultural implements, farm houses and wells.

5. Imputed rent of owner-occupied houses.

However, the following are excluded from the definition of production: (a) domestic services rendered within the household by housewives and other family members, (b) leisure time activities such as growing fruits, flowers and vegetables in the kitchen gardens, painting the house, repairing electrical appliances and household furniture.

Production of goods is counted at the point of production. Production of services is counted when they are rendered and trading services are counted at the point of sale.

Production Boundary

The concept of production boundary is useful to understand the difference between intermediate goods and final goods. Production boundary is an imaginary boundary within which production of goods and services goes on continuously. In other words, production boundary is the notional dividing line between the productive activities (those carried on inside the productive sector) and all other economic activities (such as transfer payments).

As long as the goods remain within the imaginary production boundary they are usually treated as intermediate goods. They become final goods the moment they cross the production boundary to reach the consumers. Activities giving rise to intermediate products (or intermediate transactions) take place inside the production boundary and the intermediate products to which they give rise do not cross the boundary.

The concept of production boundary is relevant because intermediate goods do not cross this boundary whereas final goods do. It may be recalled that only final goods are included in national product.

Production Function

A production function explains the technological relationship between inputs and output.

$P = f(F_1, F_2, ... F_n)$

In the above, P is the quantity of production and F_1, F_2, ... F_n are the quantities of different factors of production. Modern economists emphasise the importance of labour (L) and capital (K) in the production process. Land as a factor of production is considered unimportant or as a part of capital and thus ignored. Therefore, the simplified production function becomes:

$P = f(L, K)$

The relationship between inputs and output can be studied in two ways: (a) what happens to output as more of the variable factor is applied to a given quantity of the fixed factor. This is the study of the Law of Diminishing Returns (q.v.). It is also called the law of variable proportions. (b) What happens to output when all inputs are increased in a given proportion. This is the study of the laws of Returns to Scale (q.v.).

Production Indifference Curve See Production Isoquant

Production Possibility Curve

A production possibility curve (also called transformation curve) depicts different combinations of goods a firm can produce while using all its resources efficiently with the best available technology. At the macro level, it shows the maximum possible output of two commodities which can be produced in an economy at a point of time with the help of given factors of production, when all the resources are devoted to their production. A country cannot produce at any point over and above it because that is beyond its reach as far as availability of resources is concerned. Any movement along the curve shows how much of one commodity will have to be sacrificed to produce additional units of another commodity. It helps in knowing the opportunity cost of production of different commodities.

Production Process

Production of goods and services requires inputs. The entrepreneur combines these inputs and puts them to work. The process of combining the inputs, utilising their services and producing goods and services is called the *production process*. The inputs are also called *factors of production*. These are divided into four categories: land, labour, capital and enterprise. Wages, rent, interest and profit are called factor payments or factor incomes. Production process involves the following three elements:

1. Factors of production, viz. land, labour, capital and enterprise.

2. Combining factors of production and utilising their services.

3. Resultant production of goods and services.

The production process goes on continuously. If we want to live and prosper, we must get goods and services to satisfy our wants. Since goods and services are produced through production process, the latter becomes essential for human existence. It is the production process which makes possible the three vital flows of an economy, viz. production, consumption and investment.

An examination of the working of an economy shows that there are three main sectors: agriculture, industry and services where production goes on continuously. All the three sectors are dependent on one another. For example, agricultural sector supplies raw materials (cotton, sugarcane) to industries to produce finished products (cloth, sugar). Evidently, industrial sector is dependent on agricultural sector both for its inputs and output. In turn, agricultural sector also depends on industrial sector for machines, fertilisers etc. In between the two, there is the service sector which helps them to exchange their inputs and output by rendering services like transportation, banking and insurance. Thus, all the three sectors are interdependent and the absence of any one sector will have serious repercussions on the economy. Hence, production, exchange and consumption are essential and continuous processes of an economy.

Professional Tax

It is a kind of registration fee for practising a profession. In India, State Governments are empowered to levy a tax on professions. However, according to Article 276 of the Constitution, the total amount payable in respect of any one person to the State by way of such tax is not to exceed Rs. 2,500 per annum.

Profit

Entrepreneur is a special factor of production. He combines and organises other factors of production. The reward for his services is called profit. Profit is a residual income after other factors have been paid. Unlike the rewards of other factors of production, profit can be negative (i.e. loss).

Gross profit is defined as all gains made by an entrepreneur in the conduct of his business. Net profit is the difference between gross profit and the sum of implicit wages and interest on entrepreneur's own labour and capital.

Economists have given various explanations for the emergence of profit. Scme important explanations are described below.

Uncertainty-bearing Theory of Profit: It was propounded by American economist Frank Knight (1885-1962). To understand it, a distinction is drawn between two types of risk: (a) insurable risks and (b) non-insurable risks (uncertainties).

Every entrepreneur faces business risks like fire and theft. However, these risks can be insured against and therefore they are insurable risks. By paying premium to insurance company such risks can be avoided. The premium paid for fire insurance becomes an element of the cost of production.

However, certain risks associated with business enterprise cannot be insured against. Such non-insurable risks are called uncertainties. Profit is a reward for bearing uncertainties of business. What are these uncertainties? These uncertainties pertain to decisions regarding new products, new work methods, advertising campaigns etc. No entrepreneur can be sure about the future demand of his product or the success of his advertising campaign. No insurance company can provide insurance against such uncertainties. The entrepreneur has to trust his own judgement and he always runs the risk of misjudging market conditions. According to Frank Knight, profit is a reward for bearing non-insurable risks (or uncertainties).

Innovations Theory of Profit: According to American economist Joseph Schumpeter (1883-1950), profit is a reward for resorting to innovations. An innovation may take the form of introduction of an improved kind of machine, a new work method, exploitation of a new source of raw material and discovery of a new market. Any entrepreneur who introduces innovation derives advantage compared to his rivals.

Profit is the cause of innovations and if the innovations are successful, they result in profit. Therefore, Schumpeter believed that profit is at once both the cause as well as the effect of innovations. Profit accrues not to him who conceives the idea of innovation, nor to him who finances it but to him who introduces it.

Profit resulting from the introduction of an innovation is not permanent. After sometime an innovation is no longer novel and its advantages are known to many other entrepreneurs in the trade. Once this happens, the profit will disappear. However, a new innovation may be introduced giving rise to a new source of profit. Thus, Schumpeter maintained that innovational profit has a tendency to appear and disappear.

Dynamic Theory of Profit: The dynamic theory of profit was propounded by J. B. Clark (1847-1938), another American economist. It is based on the distinction between a static and a dynamic economy. According to Clark, there is nothing uncertain and nothing is left to chance in a static economy. In such an economy, economic activities of the previous year are repeated without change. Entrepreneurs are fully aware of the demand conditions, techniques of production and all other information regarding the operation of the economy. In a static economy like this there is neither a possibility of profit nor loss.

However, a static economy of the type described above is only a theoretical possibility. The real world is dynamic in the sense that factors which influence demand and supply change continuously. Clark mentioned the following changes which make an economy dynamic: (a) increase or decrease in population, (b) increase or decrease in the stock of capital, (c) improvement in the technique of production, (d) change in the needs of the consumers and (e) change in the methods of industrial organisation. These changes are pre-requisites for the emergence of profit. Clark believed that profit belongs essentially to economic dynamics.

Progressive Tax

A tax schedule is said to be progressive if the ratio of tax to income increases as one moves up the income scale.

Progressive taxes are more equitable because they are levied according to the ability-to-pay. They are a means to redistribute income power as they place the main burden of taxation on upper income groups. Progressive taxes not only reduce the absolute but also the relative gap between two taxpayers. For example, if 40 per cent rate applies to taxable income of Rs. 80,000 and 20 per cent to taxable income of Rs. 40,000, the post-tax incomes of the two individuals are reduced to Rs. 48,000 and Rs. 32,000 respectively. The gap in absolute terms is narrowed from Rs. 40,000 to Rs. 16,000 and the relative distance is also reduced from 2:1 to 1.5 : 1.

Besides equity considerations, tax progressivity is helpful for stabilisation policies. Under a progressive income tax, the revenue is elastic if all incomes grow proportionately. Information on the degree of progression is useful to quantify the automatic stabilisation characteristics of a tax system.

The opponents of progressive tax hold that too great a degree of progression discourages effort and risk-taking. See also Proportional Tax; and Regressive Tax.

Prohibitive Tariff

When the tariff on imports is sufficient to expand domestic production to a point where it satisfies fully the domestic demand and imports cease to be there, it is called prohibitive tariff. In this case, revenue from import tariff becomes zero. Alternatively, one can say it is a very high rate of import duty, so high that the imported commodity is priced much above the price of a similar domestically produced commodity. Prohibitive duties are imposed to protect domestic producers against ruinous foreign competition or to retaliate against similar action by another country.

Propensity to Consume

Propensity to consume (or average propensity to consume) is defined as total consumption expenditure divided by total income, i.e. C/Y. This Keynesian concept asserts that as a person's income increases, although he will spend more money on consumption than before, it will be a smaller proportion of his income. In other words, his propensity to consume grows weaker which *ipso facto* means his propensity to save grows stronger. This proposition is basic to the Keynesian Economics (q.v.).

Marginal Propensity to Consume (MPC): It refers to the extra expenditure associated with an extra amount of income. In other words, it is the proportion of each new increment of income that is spent on consumption, i.e. $\triangle C/\triangle Y$. MPC gets smaller as incomes get larger. At very low levels of income consumption may actually exceed income, i.e. people will draw on their past savings or borrow to buy what they most urgently need. See also Consumption Function; and Propensity to Save.

Propensity to Save

Propensity to save (or average propensity to save) is defined as total saving divided by total income, i.e. S/Y. Marginal propensity to save refers to the extra saving associated with an extra amount of income, i.e. $\triangle S/\triangle Y$. See also Propensity to Consume.

Property Tax

Stated comprehensively, the base for property tax should include such items as land and buildings thereon, securities, jewellery, durable consumer goods, cash etc. These items form the base for Wealth Tax (q.v.). In practice, property tax has remained confined to the value of land and buildings thereon. This tax is generally levied on *ad valorem* basis and the revenue derived therefrom is meant for local governments. The tax is expressed as some percentage of the assessed value of property. In the case of rented property, property taxes can be shifted, at least partially, through raising of rent charged.

Proportional Tax

A tax schedule is said to be proportional if the ratio of tax to income remains constant as one moves up the income scale.

A proportional rate does have redistributive effects but not as sharp as a progressive rate. For example, a 30 per cent flat rate which applies to taxable incomes of Rs. 80,000, and Rs. 40,000 reduces the post-tax incomes of the two persons to Rs. 56,000, and Rs. 28,000 respectively. The gap in absolute terms is narrowed from Rs. 40,000 to Rs. 28,000 but the relative distance remains unchanged at 2:1. See also Progressive Tax; and Regressive Tax.

Protection

It refers to government attempt to shield the domestic producers from relatively cheaper/technically superior imports so that production within the economy does not suffer due to competition. Main instruments of protection are tariff, quota, exchange control and direct intervention.

Protectionism

This term is used to describe any action by a government to alter the flows of international trade. This may be done by taxing or otherwise limiting imports.

The classical economists believed that any such intervention reduces global economic welfare. International trade, freely conducted among nations without governmental intervention, allows regional producers to specialise in the production of goods and services in which the region possesses comparative advantage. The resulting international specialisation assures optimal use of world's limited resources.

However, individual countries can in some cases benefit from protectionism. One such case is embodied in the optimal tariff argument which states that in the absence of retaliation by its trading partners, a country can gain advantage by imposing a limited tariff on imports. A second case relates to infant industries. It is argued that in order to create competitive firms in new industries, governments must temporarily protect these firms from international competition. Protection is to be granted only for as long as it takes the firm to learn the technologies and management skills required to compete.

Protectionism takes many forms. Through tariffs and nontariff barriers foreign goods and services are kept out of domestic market. Similarly, subsidies to domestic firms prove disadvantageous to foreign competitors.

The absence of protectionism is termed free trade wherein goods and services flow across international boundaries on the primary basis of comparative advantage.

Public Corporation

A public corporation is created by a special law defining its objectives, powers, and privileges. Except for appropriations to provide capital or to cover losses, it is usually independently financed. It derives revenues from the sale of goods and services and can also borrow from the Government and from the public. Employees of a public corporation are not civil servants.

Public Debt

Public debt is a method by which governments obtain money. Public debts are incurred through public loans. A loan may be either voluntary or compulsory. A government may raise loans either internally or externally. Clearly, external loans are voluntary in nature. Public loans may be for short, medium or long period. Short-term loans are also known as *floating debt*. Long term loans are also called *funded debt*.

Public borrowings involve problems of debt management which is clearly related to monetary policy. The payment of interest on and the repayment of principal of public debt (debt servicing) form part of public expenditure. Public debts, unlike taxes, leave behind liabilities for future generations.

Public Economics

It deals with the study of public bodies in the broadest sense, i.e. government at all levels, public sector enterprises and public utilities.

Public Finance

It is the study of the nature and effects of taxation, spending and borrowing policies of a government. It also includes the study of financial relations between different tiers of government in a federal polity.

Systematic study of public finance as a subject can be traced back to the publication of *Wealth of Nations* by Adam Smith in 1776. Adam Smith (1723-1790), the leader of the classical economists, devoted a whole section, viz. Book V to the study of 'the revenue of the sovereign or Commonwealth.' This in turn he divided into three chapters. The first chapter 'the expenses of the sovereign or Commonwealth' examines the different kinds of public expenditure and the appropriate means of defraying them. The second chapter, 'the sources of the general or public revenue of the society' deals with classification of revenues into various categories and also propounds the four famous Canons of Taxation (q.v.). The third chapter, 'public debts' describes the origin and history of public debt and suggests measures to reduce it.

Followers of Adam Smith devoted considerable thought to the study of public finance. Thus, David Ricardo (1772-1823) titled his main work as *The Principles of Political Economy and Taxation* (1817). Similarly, John Stuart Mill (1806-1873), the last of the classical economists, also gave respectable place to public finance in his *Principles of Political Economy* (1848). There was no major contribution to the subject of public finance during the second half of the 19th century.

Interest in the study of public finance was revived with the beginning of the 20th century when there appeared a couple of books specifically devoted to public finance. Two such books of the same title stand out distinctly: *Public Finance* (1922) by Hugh Dalton (1887-1962) and *Public Finance* (1928) by A.C. Pigou (1877-1959). The publication of *The General Theory of Employment, Interest and Money* (1936) by John Maynard Keynes (1883-1946) gave a new impetus and importance to the subject of public finance.

Should public debt be included in the study of public finance? Considerable disagreement prevails among economists on this question. One view is that public borrowing is a form of raising resources for the government and therefore its inclusion in public finance is perfectly logical. The other view is that public debt involves considerations of interest rates and related matters which belong more to monetary theory than fiscal policy. As a via media, public debt is discussed in fiscal policy only from the angle of government receipts.

Purchasing Power Parity Adjusted Exchange Rate See Exchange Rate

Purchasing Power Parity Theory

Propounded by Gustav Cassel (1866-1944), this theory states that the rate of exchange of two currencies can be better determined by the price levels in the two countries, i.e. rate of exchange can be set where the purchasing power of the two currencies are equal to each other. Any change in exchange rate can also be explained in terms of changes in price levels from a given base level when the balance of payments was in adjustment. If prices in a country rise by 10 per cent, the external value of the currency falls by 10 per cent and vice versa.

Q

Quality of Life

It refers to the living conditions of the people of a country. Living conditions are judged by the availability of health, educational and other basic facilities of life. It also includes economic opportunities available to the people and their ability to take advantage of these opportunities.

Quantity Theory of Money See Equation of Exchange

Quasi Rent

The notion of rent is traditionally associated with land which is fixed in supply in the short-run as well as in the long-run. No other factor is fixed in supply like land. However, there can be factors which are fixed in supply in the short-run though not in the long-run. Such factors, according to British economist Alfred Marshall (1842-1924), can be "machines and other appliances made by man." These are not fixed in supply like land and hence earnings from their use cannot be called rent. However, their supply is fixed in the short-run because it takes time to duplicate them. Their fixity of supply in the short-run makes them akin, though not identical, to land. Their reward in the short-run is a kind of rent for which he coined the term *quasi rent*. See also Rent.

Quick Succession Relief

It means a reduction in Estate Duty (q.v.) if it is paid twice within a few years on the same estate due to a second death. An estate which has been subjected to duty may change hands quickly on account of successive deaths and again become liable to payment of duty. In such cases, estate duty puts undue burden on families suffering deaths at short intervals. This problem is mitigated by providing quick succession relief in the law.

Quota

It fixes a limit on the amount of a particular item that may be exported/imported during a given period of time. As an instrument of trade policy, quotas provide more effective protection for domestic producers than a comparably restrictive tariff. However, quotas do not generate additional tax revenue.

Quotient System

Under this system, the incomes of husband and wife are aggregated and then subjected to a rate schedule which differs from the schedule for single persons. Let us suppose a basic tax rate of 20 per cent operates on an income above Rs. 40,000 and rises to 30 per cent when taxable income exceeds Rs. 55,000. A quotient of 1.5 would imply that a couple would pay 20 per cent tax on joint income in excess of Rs. 60,000 and reach the 30 per cent rate only when their income is above Rs. 82,500. Clearly, the effect of this system depends on the figure which is chosen as the quotient. Thus, a quotient of 1 amounts to simple aggregation of the two incomes. A quotient of 2 ensures that no couple loses and most gain a tax advantage by marriage, whatever their incomes. The more unequal their incomes, the larger the tax benefit. This system of taxation operates in France.

R

Random Variable **See Variable**

Ratchet Effect

When commodity taxes (excise duties and sales taxes) are reduced on some goods and increased on others, there is a tendency on the part of traders not to lower prices of the former category of goods, and to increase prices of the latter category of goods to allow for additional taxation. The prices move only upwards and the tendency is analogous to the mechanical working of a ratchet which moves only in one direction.

Rationality

Economics deals with the behaviour of rational human beings. The assumption of rationality is at the core of economic analysis. Thus, a consumer must try to maximise his satisfaction while a producer must try to maximise his profit.

Real Cost **See Cost of Production**

Real Interest **See Interest**

Real Wages **See Wages**

Recession

It means a substantial drop in the level of economic activities in an economy.

Recessionary Gap

It is a situation in which actual national income of a country falls short of its potential national income.

Reciprocal Demand Curve **See Offer Curve**

Reciprocal Trade Agreements

Agreements under which participating countries agree on certain mutual conditions such as imports in exchange of exports, cut in tariff as done by the other signatory country.

Re-export

It refers to export of previously imported goods without additional processing or alteration. If they remain at a Free Port (q.v.) or Bonded Warehouse (q.v.), such goods usually are not subject to duty.

Refund of Tax

Refund means to pay back. Where the amount of tax paid by a person in respect of any assessment year exceeds the amount of tax properly assessable for that year, he is entitled to a refund of such excess tax paid.

Regression

Economic analysis is mainly concerned with relationship among variables. Relationship between price and demand (demand function), output and cost (cost function), input and output (production function) and many others are familiar to students of economics. To pin down these relationships among economic variables to statistical interpretation, the techniques of correlation and regression are used. If hypotheses concerning relationships are empirically verified (with the help of data from the real world) again and again, they become economic laws like the law of demand or the law of diminishing marginal returns.

Correlation and Regression: In introductory statistics, great deal of attention is devoted to making inferences about one variable (univariate analysis) e.g. finding its mean, standard deviation etc. Economists are typically less interested in describing one variable (say demand) in isolation. They are more interested in describing the relationship between variables (bivariate/multivariate analysis), e.g. relationship between income and consumption of an individual.

Correlation analysis shows the degree to which variables are related. Regression analysis shows how variables are related. Simple correlation analysis yields only one number, an index designed to give an immediate picture of how closely two variables move together. In regression analysis, a whole mathematical function is estimated (i.e. the regression equation). In correlation analysis, cause and effect relations are not stated. For example, correlation between X and Y can be estimated regardless of whether X affects Y or vice versa. Because it is their business to define cause and effect relationships, economists find correlation a less powerful technique. For the description of relationship between variables, regression is a popular and useful technique.

Regression equations (also known as estimating equations), are algebraic expressions of the regression line. Let us take into account two variables, viz. consumption (C) and income (Y). The regression line of C on Y will give the most probable values of C for given values of Y. The regression equation of C on Y is expressed as follows:

$C = a + bY$

In this equation, C is the dependent variable and Y the independent variable. Or, we may call them explained variable and explanatory variable respectively. A variable is called dependent because it is supposed to be functionally dependent on the other variable. The regression model attempts to explain observed changes in a dependent variable as being caused by changes in the independent variable. Conceptually, changes in the independent variable are observed independently of the causal relation expressed by the model.

In the equation, a and b are constants which determine the position and slope of the regression line respectively. If the values of a and b are obtained the regression line is completely determined. These values are obtained by the method of least squares. The line thus obtained is known as the line of best fit.

Regressive Tax

A tax schedule is said to be regressive if the ratio of tax to income declines as one moves up the income scale.

A regressive tax increases the relative gap between two individuals but keeps the absolute distance unchanged. For example, if a fixed amount tax of Rs. 500 is levied on taxable incomes of Rs. 2,000 and Rs. 1,000, the post-tax incomes of the two individuals are reduced to Rs. 1,500 and Rs. 500 respectively. The gap in absolute terms remains unchanged but the relative distance is increased from 2:1 to 3:1.

A tax which is technically proportional in terms of the tax base can often be considered regressive in terms of the taxpayer's income. Thus, an excise duty of Rs. 2 per kilogram of sugar will entail a tax burden of Rs. 4 each on Mr. A and Mr. B if they each buy 2 kilograms of sugar. *Prima facie,* the tax may appear proportional but if it is related to their differing income levels, it will turn out to be regressive. In percentage terms, the amount of tax imposes a larger burden on the poor man than on the rich man, aggravating inequalities of income. Indirect taxes are often regressive though it is difficult to measure the degree of regressivity. See also Progressive Tax; and Proportional Tax.

Regrettable Costs See Economic Development and Economic Welfare

Relative Income Hypothesis See Consumption Function

Rent

Land is a factor of production and the reward for its services is called rent.

Ricardian Theory of Rent: Noted English classical economist David Ricardo (1772-1823) examined in detail the nature of rent on land. He wrote in the early 19th century when rents were high owing to Napoleonic wars. Ricardo defined rent as "that portion of the produce of the earth which is paid to the landlord for the use of the original and indestructible powers of the soil". Ricardo distinguished between (a) scarcity rent and (b) differential rent.

Scarcity Rent: If all land on an island is homogeneous and freely available, no rent will arise. When all land is fully occupied and demand for land still increases, rent will occur. The amount of this rent will be determined by the demand for land and the supply of land. If there is perfect competition among landlords as well as tenants, and all land is homogeneous then all the farmers will pay the same rent. The occurrence of rent or an increase in rent will not change the supply of land. Once fully occupied, land has zero elasticity of supply in the short-run as well as in the long-run. Thus, scarcity rent results from the scarcity of homogeneous land. Ricardo maintained that high rents are not a sign of the bounty of nature. Contrarily, they indicate niggardliness of nature.

Differential Rent: Scarcity rent arises when land is both homogeneous and scarce. It is unrealistic to assume that all pieces of land are homogeneous. In fact, different tracts of land differ not only in fertility but also in terms of location. Differences in fertility cause differential rents. Rent is different on each grade of land: superior the land, higher is the rent and vice versa. The grade of land which is just worth cultivating is called marginal land.

In the early years of the 19th century, prices of corn (cereals) were ruling high in Britain and there was a great debate about it. Some people believed that corn prices were high because landlords were charging high rents from the farmers. High rents were the cause for high prices of corn. Ricardo and his followers did not agree with this reasoning and held the opposite view. They believed that the price of corn was high due to shortages caused by Napoleonic wars and also because of increasing pressure of population. Since the price of corn was high it was more profitable to grow corn and therefore competition among the farmers to obtain land from the landlords. This competition led to high rents paid for the use of land. Thus, the famous dictum: *Corn is high not because rent is high: rent is high because corn is high.*

Modern Theory of Rent: According to modern economists, notably British economist Mrs. Joan Robinson (1903-1983), rent is a surplus which can be earned by any factor of production. It is called *economic rent.*

Every employed factor of production has some actual earning, i.e. earning in its present job. It also has a *transfer earning*, i.e. earning in its next best use or job. In other words, the amount that a factor must earn in its present use to avoid moving or transferring to another use is called its transfer earning. Economic rent is a surplus earned by a factor of production over and above its transfer earning. It is the difference between its actual and transfer earning.

Economic rent = Actual earning - Transfer earning.

What determines economic rent? In most cases, actual earning of a factor of production is composed of transfer earning and economic rent. In other words, actual earning can be divided between transfer earning and economic rent. The manner of this division depends on the supply position of the factor in question. The various possibilities with a given demand but varying supply conditions are as follows:

If the supply is perfectly inelastic the whole of actual earning is economic rent. A perfectly inelastic supply implies that same quantity will be supplied even if price falls to zero. It means the transfer earnings are zero and whatever is being earned in the present job is a surplus or economic rent.

If the supply is perfectly elastic, the actual earning is equal to transfer earning and hence economic rent is zero. A perfectly elastic supply implies that even a small decrease in actual earning would cause all units of the factor to move elsewhere. Perfectly inelastic and perfectly elastic supply conditions are extreme situations. Usually, the supply curve is positively sloped. It means an increase in the price of the factor attracts more units into that employment. However, the same increase provides additional earnings to already employed units of the factor though they are willing to work at prices prevailing before the increase. Thus, rise in the price of the factor increases economic rent of all units of the factor already in employment. See also Quasi Rent.

Repo See Repurchase Option

Representative Tax System

It is a measure of Fiscal Capacity (q.v.) of a state government. The yield of the representative tax system is the amount of revenue that would be raised if a state government taxed all potential tax bases at national average rates.

Repurchase Option (Repo)

Under a Repo transaction, a holder of securities sells them to an investor with an agreement to repurchase at a pre-determined date and rate.

Reserves

It is the money from profits not paid as dividend and which is retained by a company to be used later for purposes which the directors think fit.

Residential Status

In the tax laws of most countries, income which is subject to charge of tax varies according to the residential status of a taxpayer. There are elaborate rules for ascertaining the residential status of an assessee. Generally, a resident taxpayer is charged to income tax on his world income, subject to a double taxation relief in respect of foreign incomes taxed abroad. However, a non-resident is charged tax only on incomes received, accruing, or arising in that country.

Resident of a Country

A resident is defined as a person who ordinarily resides in a country and whose centre of interest lies in that country. Since he normally lives in the country of his interest, he is called a normal resident of that country. The term normal resident covers both individuals and institutions. The following are not resident individuals: (a) foreign visitors on holidays, medical treatment, study tours, conferences, sports events etc., (b) crew members of foreign vessels, (c) officials, diplomats of a foreign country, (d) employees of international organisations who are not the citizens of the country in which the offices are located.

Restraint of Trade

It is a legal concept used with reference to antitrust policy. Its classic expression is found in the US Sherman Antitrust Act of 1890: "Every contract, combination in the form of trust or otherwise, or conspiracy in restraint of trade or commerce among the several states, or with foreign nations, is declared to be illegal." Trade is restrained when persons or business firms agree by contract to (a) limit competition among themselves, (b) prevent others from competing, (c) seek such limitations by a merger of actual or potential competitors. Anticompetitive agreements, mergers and collusions are unacceptable in a society built on free enterprise and free competition.

Returns to Scale

This law pertains to production situation under which all factors of production can be increased in a given proportion. By assuming that all factors are variable, the law deals with long-run variations in output. Only two factors of production, viz. labour and capital are taken into account.

If there is an increase or decrease in labour and capital in a given proportion, the scale of production is changed. What is the relationship between increase in factors of production and the consequent increase in output? There are three dimensions of returns to scale. They are the following :

Increasing Returns to Scale: This is a situation where if factors are increased in a given proportion, output increases in a greater proportion. For example, if labour and capital are doubled, output is more than doubled.

What is the explanation for increasing returns to scale? The main reason for increasing returns to scale lies in the advantages of division of labour and specialisation. Higher scale of production facilitates greater division of labour and specialisation and as a result labour productivity increases. Large scale of production generates various types of *economies of scale* or *internal economies* for the firm. These are: technological economies, managerial economies, financial economies and marketing economies. The firm also overcomes the problem of indivisibility of specialised and costly machines.

Constant Returns to Scale: This case refers to that situation where if factors are increased in a given proportion, the output also increases in the same proportion. For example, if capital and labour are doubled, the output is also doubled. We may come across such a production situation in real life. If one worker working on a machine produces 5 units of a commodity, it can be expected that two workers working on two identical machines will produce 10 units of the commodity.

Decreasing Returns to Scale: If factors of production are increased in a given proportion and output increases in a smaller proportion, it will be a situation of decreasing returns.

There are various reasons for the operation of decreasing returns. As the firm goes on expanding its size, it becomes increasingly difficult to co-ordinate and properly manage the activities of various departments of the firm. The firm may find it difficult to procure more and more raw material or finance for its production process. Marketing of the finished product may also become difficult. Excessive use of machines may result in more wear and tear. All these disadvantages put together are termed as *diseconomies of scale* or *internal diseconomies* which are related to the expanding size of the firm.

It is noteworthy that whereas all other factors of production can be purchased from the market and therefore increased but the services of the entrepreneur himself are fixed. There are limits on the supervisory and decision-making capabilities of the entrepreneur. If we assume the services of an entrepreneur as fixed while other factors are progressively increased, the law of decreasing returns to scale turns out to be a special case of the law of variable proportions.

In short, a firm normally experiences increasing returns to scale in the initial stages of its production, constant returns to scale at medium level and decreasing returns at very high levels of production.

Revealed Preference

Indifference curve analysis explains consumer behaviour in terms of scales of preference set out in the form of indifference curves. Many economists doubt if consumers can order their preferences precisely and rationally. Alternatively, revealed preference theory of demand observes what the consumers actually do when they make their purchases. Since a consumer reveals the nature of his preferences, the analysis is known as revealed preference. American economist Paul Samuelson introduced the term revealed preference in 1938. Revealed preference theory is claimed to be superior to indifference curve analysis because it allows econometricians to test their hypotheses. With the advancement of mathematical techniques, there is a strong preference among economists to deal with hypotheses which are statistically testable.

It is assumed that a consumer has a given income to spend. He is faced with various alternative combinations of two goods (X and Y) which he can afford to buy. He will choose that combination which he ranks highest.

Strong Versus Weak Ordering: As opposed to indifference curve technique (based on weak ordering), revealed preference assumes strong ordering. If a set of items is strongly ordered, then each item has its own definite place in that order as, for example, letters in the alphabet. Conversely, under weak ordering ranking may not be possible for some items in the set. In other words, some of the items may have to be clubbed at one place. For example, all combinations of commodities A and B on an indifference curve give the consumer the same level of satisfaction. This is weak ordering. However, the indifference curves themselves are strongly ordered.

Two-term Consistency and Transitivity: These are other elements of revealed preference theory. Two-term consistency ensures that any two items in a ranking are consistently placed to each other. If A is preferred to B, then B cannot be preferred to A. Symbolically, if A>B, then B A. Consistent ordering also requires transitivity. Thus, if a consumer prefers A combination to B combination, and also prefers B combination to C combination, the transitivity condition requires that he prefers A combination to C combination. Symbolically,

If A > B and B > C, then A > C.

The fundamental difference between the two approaches is that while indifference curve analysis explains price effect through income and substitution effects, the revealed preference explains it through cost difference method.

Revenue

Profit of a firm is the difference between total revenue derived from selling its product and the cost of producing it.

Total Revenue: Total revenue means the total amount of money which a firm receives from the sale of its output. Total revenue (TR) is equal to the quantity sold (q) multiplied by the price per unit (p) of the commodity. Thus, TR = pq.

Average Revenue: Average revenue (AR) is total revenue divided by the quantity sold. Thus AR = TR/q.

Marginal Revenue: Marginal revenue (MR) is the change in total revenue resulting from an increase of 1 unit in the sale of a commodity. The marginal revenue resulting from the sale of the nth unit of a commodity is the change in total revenue when sales increase from n-1 units to n units. Symbolically, $MR = TR_n - TR_{n-1}$

Cost-output relationship is applicable to all firms irrespective of the market structure in which they operate. However, this is not so in case of revenue. In other words, there is no single theory of revenue which applies to all firms. Revenue-output relationship of a firm is governed by the market situation in which a firm operates. Thus, a firm working under perfect competition is faced with different revenue conditions than a monopoly firm.

Under perfect competition, market price of a commodity is determined by the interaction of market demand curve and market supply curve. Every firm has to sell its product at the price so determined. A firm is a price-taker and can sell any quantity of its product at the established price. Technically speaking, the marginal revenue of the firm remains the same. If marginal revenue is constant, the average revenue is also constant and equal to marginal revenue.

Monopoly exists when an industry is in the hands of a single producer. Since the firm is the only producer of its product, the demand curve it faces is the market demand curve for that product, and it slopes downward. A monopolist can choose any price-quantity combination on this curve. This curve is also the average revenue curve of the monopolist firm. In view of the negative slope of the curve, the monopolist will have to lower his price if he wishes to sell more. He can increase the price but that will lead to reduced sale.

Revenue Budget **See Budget**

Revenue Deficit

It refers to the excess of revenue expenditure over revenue receipts.

Revenue deficit = Revenue receipts - Revenue expenditure

Revenue deficit represents dissaving on government account, and hence the use of the savings of the other sectors of the economy to finance a part of the consumption expenditure of the government. In fact, fiscal policy should ensure surplus in the revenue budget so that government also contributes to savings in the economy.

Revenue Expenditure

It relates to the normal running of an organisation. Broadly speaking, all those expenditures of an organisation which do not result in the creation of physical or financial assets are treated as revenue expenditures. See also Capital Expenditure.

Revenue Receipts

Moneys obtained in the normal course of business are called revenue receipts, e.g. sale proceeds, interest on deposits, and dividends on investment. Revenue receipts are normally of recurring nature and are not meant for any specific purpose. See also Capital Receipts.

Revenue Sharing

It is a term used in the context of fiscal federalism whereby a higher level of government imposes and collects certain taxes but shares, permissively or mandatorily, the proceeds with lower level governments. See also Tax Sharing.

Ricardian Theory of Rent See Rent

Road Tax See Motor Vehicle Tax

Runaway Capital

It refers to that investment which is made abroad instead of at home. It, therefore, involves loss to the domestic economy in terms of employment and income generation. Multinational corporations are often accused of encouraging this type of investment. See also Job Exports.

Rybczynski Theorem

In a two country, two commodity, two factor model of free trade, any autonomous increase in the supply of a single factor of production (say labour) in a country reduces its price and that of the commodities which use this factor intensively. With the rise in production of labour-intensive commodities on the one hand and fall in their prices due to fall in wage rate, it is likely that their exports will lead to worsening of a country's external terms of trade.

This theorem propounded by T. M. Rybczynski is based on the assumptions of a linear homogeneous production function and a constant marginal rate of substitution.

S

Sales Tax

It is normally an *ad valorem* levy imposed on the seller with reference to the transaction of sale. Sales tax is generally regressive in nature because being paid by all consumers, it takes a larger proportion of small incomes than of larger ones. On the basis of the stage of collection, sales tax is classified into (a) multi-point sales tax and (b) single-point sales tax.

Multi-point Sales Tax: As a multi-point levy, sales tax may be applied at two or more stages of production and distribution and becomes akin to a turnover tax applicable at each transaction of purchase and sale. Multi-stage sales tax is politically expedient because a given amount of revenue can be raised at a lower rate of taxation which also reduces the temptation for tax evasion.

The chief demerit of multi-point sales tax is its encouragement to vertical integration of production and distribution processes. Thus, it discriminates against non-integrated firms. Producers of finished products prefer to produce their own materials and components, and this tendency harms the interest of independent suppliers, particularly small ones. Furthermore, multi-point sales tax discriminates against those goods, and their consumers, which have to pass through numerous transactions. In view of these disadvantages, John Due has opined, "On administrative as well as economic and equity grounds the objections to the multi-stage form are so great as to suggest its complete rejection, regardless of circumstances."

Single-point Sales Tax: A single-point sales tax applies to one stage, either at the manufacturing or the wholesale or the retail level. At manufacturing level, sales tax applies to sale by manufacturer of the finished product and is similar to excise duty. At the wholesale level, the tax applies to the last wholesale transaction, i.e. purchase by the retailer. The retail sales tax applies to the final sale which means sale to the consumer.

The main advantage of single-point sales tax is that it does not discriminate against non-integrated firms as does multi-point sales tax. Thus, it discourages vertical integration and promotes horizontal integration. As regards the stage of its imposition, the retail stage is considered the most satisfactory due to the following reasons.

1. Sales tax at the retail stage is collected when final sale to the consumer takes place. Thus, it avoids what economists call *cascading* or *pyramiding* effect of a tax. The contention is that middlemen apply fixed percentage mark up to purchase prices and if the purchase prices include taxes (as is the case if sales tax is imposed at manufacturer's or wholesaler's level), the mark up will be applicable to the tax component of the purchase prices as well, a situation which must be avoided in the interest of consumers.

2. A given revenue can be realised by applying a lower tax rate at the retail stage as compared to other stages because the margins of all middlemen are included at the final stage of sale, thereby meaning an enlargement of the tax base at the retail stage.

3. The desired change in the ratio of tax to consumer expenditure can be achieved more effectively in case of retail stage sales tax. This will be difficult at *other stages* because the margins of dealers on various goods, besides

being applied to the tax component of the purchase prices, may differ significantly.

4. Sales tax at the retail stage can be shown separately from the price and thus made known to the purchaser, increasing tax consciousness among taxpayers.

5. Expected changes in the rates of retail sales tax do not lead to changes in inventory position of the firms. Anticipated changes in the rates of sales tax at *other stages* may influence inventory decisions of the firms causing dislocation in trade circles.

However, retail stage sales tax has its own problems, the chief being the large number of taxpayers in the form of small shopkeepers and scattered retail outlets. In developing countries, the problem of tax administration is more acute in view of widespread illiteracy, lack of monetisation and poor accounting practices. From the administrative viewpoint, this form of taxation is costlier and cumbersome, offering ample scope for tax evasion and corruption.

Sales tax at the manufacturing or wholesale stage is administratively preferable because the number of taxpayers is small and readily identifiable. However, the problem of *cascading* will reappear. In fact, the farther we move from the retail level, the more serious the problem of *cascading* becomes. In short, the problem boils down to a trade off between economic rationale and administrative efficiency. The relative weightage to competing objectives depends on political judgement and the economic circumstances under which the sales tax system has to operate.

Savings

Importance of domestic savings in developing economies is well-known. Domestic savings comprise government and non-government savings. Government savings are defined as budget balance on revenue account which means an excess of revenue receipts over revenue expenditure. Non-government savings, consisting of household savings, and business savings, account for a major share of total savings.

Say's Law

Say's law, a proposition propounded by French classical economist Jean Baptiste Say (1767-1832), maintains that every supply creates its own demand. This proposition occupied an important place in the thinking of classical economists. Say believed that aggregate supply of goods produced is the same thing as the aggregate demand. In other words, total demand and total supply are identical. His reasoning was as follows:

In the course of producing goods, business firms incur money costs in the form of payments for the use of land, labour, capital and some profit for the entrepreneur. Money paid out by business firms becomes the purchasing power in the hands of different factors of production. They may either spend it in consumption or save it, putting the savings into some kind of investment goods. By this process of spending for consumption or for the purchase of investment goods, the money flows back into the hands of business firms who have these goods for sale. It follows that the recipients of money incomes must always have enough to buy all the goods produced at prices which will cover their costs. It is not possible to produce more than the people have the means to pay for. There could never be a lack of sufficient demand for all the goods that the economy could produce. Or, to put it differently, a general over-production of goods is impossible. See also Classical Economics.

Scarce Currency

Under Article VII of the Fund Charter, International Monetary Fund can declare a currency (say US dollar) scarce when its demand from member countries rises and which it is not in a position to meet. Then available supply of the currency can be rationed by it among the countries that want it. The Fund simultaneously takes steps to augment the supplies of that currency by other means such as borrowing from the market.

Scarcity Rent See Rent

Scientific Socialism See Marxism

Scrutiny Assessment

It arises where an assessing officer considers it necessary to ensure that the assessee has not (a) understated his income, (b) returned excessive loss or (c) underpaid the tax. He may serve a notice on the assessee requiring him to appear on the specified date or to furnish any document/evidence in support of his return of income.

There are various factors guiding the selection of a case for scrutiny. Some of these are: (a) continuous losses from year to year, (b) low profitability declared compared to the general profitability in similar business, (c) extraordinary expenditure booked and (d) huge private borrowings made.

Search and Seizure

The term refers to the powers of tax authorities to obtain tax-related information in the possession of a taxpayer which is not otherwise being disclosed.

Tax officials are vested with considerable powers to carry out search operations. To conduct a search and seizure (popularly called raid), an authorisation in the prescribed form is issued by the competent tax authority under his signature and seal.

Under Sections 132 and 132A of the Indian Income Tax Act, 1961, a search party can (a) enter and search any building, place or vehicle in occupation of the person being searched, (b) break the lock and examine any box, locker, cupboard etc., (c) seize any books of account, other documents, money, bullion, jewellery etc.

Second Best, Theory of

Optimality conditions given by Italian economist Vilfredo Pareto (1848-1923) require that for maximising welfare in an economy, conditions such as free trade, perfect competition must be fully satisfied. Jacob Viner (1892-1970) demonstrated that unless all the Pareto conditions are fulfilled, optimum welfare level cannot be reached. Accordingly, free trade among all the nations is the best situation. However, a customs union which provides free trade only among the member-nations is a second best situation. It is better than a no trade or restricted trade situation though it is inferior to a universal free trade situation. Thus, the theory of customs union is known as the theory of second best. See also Welfare Economics; and Customs Union.

Sectoral Productivity

Sectoral productivity is the ratio of the share of a sector in output to the share of that sector in labour force. This statistical measure is important to analyse the size and direction of change in productivity levels over time and across countries.

Secular Deterioration in Terms of Trade Hypothesis

Noted economists Raul Prebisch, Hans Singer, Hla Myint and Ragnar Nurkse have shown through their empirical and analytical works that there has been a secular deterioration in the long-term terms of trade of primary goods exporting developing countries. As a result, foreign trade, instead of being an engine of growth, has contributed to the decline in the real purchasing power of their exports. They gave the following reasons for this decline.

1. Despite improvement in productivity of manufactured goods sector of the developed countries consequent upon which the manufactured goods prices should have fallen, it has not happened due to strong trade unionism and monopoly power. Thus, the prices of manufactured goods have remained high. Conversely, labour unions in primary producing sector of LDCs are weak and whatever improvement in productivity is there has been reflected in falling wages and commodity prices.

2. Even during a trade cycle, prices of manufactured goods do not fall as trade union and monopolists do not let prices fall. However, in case of primary goods, a depression takes away any gain earned during upswing because prices are more flexible especially downwards.

3. Demand for primary products in rich countries has fallen due to the operation of Engel's Law (q.v.) which states that as income rises, expenditure on agricultural goods does not rise to the same extent, leaving a lesser proportion of income spent on them.

4. Technological progress has also reduced the demand for primary goods as, for example, availability of synthetic products.

5. There has been a growing trend toward protectionism in the developed countries which means development of agricultural sector there itself through subsidisation and high import duties on competitive agricultural products.

Securities

The term securities includes shares, bonds, debentures etc. of any body corporate or government. Securities which appear on the official stock exchange list and which may be bought and sold on the stock exchange are called listed securities.

Sellers' Market

It is a market situation in which demand is more than supply so that sellers have a favourable bargaining position. Due to short supply, sellers can successfully charge higher prices as, for example, during wartime.

Service Taxes

Service taxes are broadly in the nature of charges for water, drainage, lighting, conservancy, fire fighting etc. They are usually collected along with, and assessed on the same basis as, property tax.

Service taxes can be levied only after the concerned service has begun to be rendered. Similarly, they can be levied only in areas where the service is in fact rendered.

Set Off of Losses See Loss Set Off

Sex Ratio

It refers to the number of females per thousand of male population in a country. The trend of sex ratio in India has been in favour of masculine population. According to the 1981 census, there were 933 females per thousand males. This is due to lack of attention and care given to female children, and the higher death-rate among women in the reproductive age. It is noteworthy that in Western countries, the sex ratio favours the feminine population.

Share Transfer

It is a transaction for the ownership of shares. A share transfer form is completed by the seller and sent with the share certificate to the company's registered office. The buyer's name is then entered in the share register. The buyer bears the cost of registration, duty on the shares and brokerage.

Shifting of Tax

It means the transfer of tax burden from the original payer to some other entity. Tax shifting is the study of ways in which the burden of taxation is shifted among persons and organisations in the economy. For example, excise duty on producers of sugar can be shifted forward to the consumers by increasing the price of the commodity by the amount of the tax. The burden of excise duty can be shifted backward also by reducing the price paid to sugarcane suppliers and other factors of production. Forward shifting or backward shifting may be full or partial.

Is it always possible for the producers to shift the burden of a commodity tax on to the consumers? In fact, the degree and the direction to which a tax can be shifted depends on a host of factors including elasticity of demand and supply, coverage of the tax, and the time period allowed for adjustments.

Elasticity of Demand and Supply: As for the elasticity factor, the general rules are: 1. Higher the elasticity of demand, greater is the tax burden on producers. 2. Higher the elasticity of supply, greater will be the tax burden on consumers. In technical terms, the ratio in which tax burden is divided between consumers and producers is given by the ratio of elasticity of supply to elasticity of demand.

Coverage of the Tax: If excise duty is imposed on tea and not on coffee, then it would be difficult for producers to shift the tax burden on tea to consumers. If they try to do so, consumers have the option to switch over to the consumption of coffee. However, if excise duty is imposed on both tea and coffee, it would be difficult for the consumers to escape the tax burden. Thus, wider the coverage of a tax, the greater will be the burden on consumers and vice versa. Hence, selective taxes are more likely to be avoided by the consumers than broad-based taxes.

Time Period: Distribution of the burden of an indirect tax between producers and consumers is governed also by the time period allowed for adjustment. In the short-run, it is difficult for the producers to adjust their supplies in response to fluctuating demand because of certain fixed costs of production. Technically, the supply curve in the short-run is less elastic. Under such circumstances, it would be difficult for the producers to pass on the tax burden to the consumers. However, in the long-run, the distinction between fixed and variable costs vanishes. Producers can adjust the supplies in tune with demand conditions. Technically, the supply curve is elastic, may be perfectly elastic. Thus, the burden of commodity tax can be passed on to the consumers.

Time factor is important from demand angle also. If a commodity is taxed, it may have to be purchased in the short-run in the absence of substitutes. However, in the long-run substitutes of the taxed commodity may become available. Moreover, consumption habits may also change. Hence, consumers are in a better position to avoid the tax in the long-run. Since both demand and supply become more elastic in the long-run, it is difficult to say as to what extent producers and consumers would be able to avoid the tax burden. See also Incidence of Taxation.

Short-run and Long-run

In economics, short-run is defined as a period of time over which certain factors of production cannot be changed. These factors are called fixed factors and usually pertain to plant, machinery, rent for buildings, insurance charges and other payments fixed by contract. In the short-run, output can be changed by employing more or less of those factors which can be varied at short notice. These are called variable factors and usually refer to labour services, raw materials, fuels etc.

The length of the short-run is not the same for all industries. In the case of a modern steel plant it may mean a period of 3 to 4 years because this is the likely time required to set up a new or expand the existing plant. Any sudden increase in the demand for steel will have to be met, to the extent possible, by employing more labour on the existing capital equipment. Conversely, short-run may mean a duration of 3 to 4 weeks for a bakery. A sudden increase in the demand for biscuits can be met adequately by employing more labour as well as installing additional oven in a few weeks. Thus, the duration of short-run is determined by technological considerations, i.e. how quickly equipment can be manufactured and installed.

Long-run is defined as a period long enough for varying any of the factors of production. Amounts of labour as well as capital (plant and machinery) can be changed according to the requirements of the firm. There are no fixed factors and therefore no fixed costs in the long-run. All factors are variable and hence all costs are variable. Thus, there is no need to separate total cost into fixed and variable categories as is the case in short-run. The absence of fixed costs is the essential characteristic of long-run which distinguishes it from short-run. In the long-run we deal with total cost and average cost without further classification. However, the concept of marginal cost is applicable to both short-run and long-run. Marginal cost refers to the change in total cost when output is increased by one unit from its present level.

In the long-run, new firms can enter and existing firms exit the industry without any difficulty. In the short-run, existing firms cannot leave in view of constraints imposed by fixed costs, and similarly new firms cannot join the industry because it takes time to set up new plants.

In the short-run, firms may earn supernormal profits or suffer losses (i.e. subnormal profits). In case they are earning supernormal profits, new firms will enter the industry to share these profits. This means, at a given price more will be supplied because there are more suppliers. Supply will increase and if market demand remains unchanged, the equilibrium price will fall.

As the equilibrium price decreases, both new and old firms will have to adjust their output to this new price. Entry of new firms will continue and so also the decrease in price. This process will go on till all firms in the industry are just earning normal profit.

Conversely, if firms are suffering losses in the short run, some of them will leave the industry in the long-run. Supply will decrease and if market demand remains unchanged, the equilibrium price will increase. Firms continue to exit and price continues to rise until the remaining firms can cover their total costs and earn normal profit.

In the context of exit from the industry, it is sometimes important to distinguish between *marginal and intramarginal firms*. A marginal firm is one which is just covering its total cost and would exit if price falls by even a small amount. An intramarginal firm is that which is earning profits and would require a larger fall in price to decide to exit.

Since long-run equilibrium is normal profit equilibrium, there is no incentive for new firms to enter the industry or for the existing firms to leave the industry.

It is pertinent to note that long-run equilibrium depicts the most efficient manner of production. The equilibrium takes place where the average cost is the minimum.

Shoup Mission

It was a tax mission headed by the American fiscal expert Carl S. Shoup which visited Japan in 1949 with the task of reorganising the tax system as a whole. It recommended a tax plan intended to achieve a thorough overhaul of the Japanese tax system. Shoup Mission recommendations placed more emphasis on direct taxes, mainly income taxes on individuals and corporations. However, the reconstructed tax system introduced under the influence of USA was of temporary duration because many of the taxes were abolished or modified soon after their enactment.

Shut-down Point

It is possible that a firm suffers losses in the short-run. In spite of incurring losses, it may prefer to remain in business. This is so because short-run is characterised by certain fixed costs which the firm must bear whether it remains in business or not. These fixed costs pertain to plant, machinery, rent for buildings, insurance charges and other payments fixed by contracts. Contrarily, there are variable costs which can be dispensed with in the short-run as, for example, labour on daily wages, raw materials, fuels etc.

It is clear that if a firm ceases operation in the short-run, its loss will be equal to fixed costs. It follows that a firm should stay in production even if it cannot cover its full fixed cost. However, there is no doubt that the firm must cover all its variable costs. As soon as the average revenue (price) becomes less than average variable cost, the firm must shut-down. In other words, a firm should produce only if total revenue is not less than total variable cost.

Single Tax Movement

American economist Henry George launched the single tax movement in the 19th century. In his book *Progress and Poverty*, he pointed out that the fixed supply of land coupled with a rapidly rising demand for it, conferred on the owners of land immense gains from the natural progress of society. Without contributing anything, landlords made huge fortunes from these unearned increments. He calculated that most government expenditure could be financed by a single tax that would take away the unearned increments of landlords. His appeal for a single tax receded gradually with the steadily increasing size of the government in modern societies.

Sinking Fund

It refers to a fund to which a debtor makes periodic contributions to facilitate retirement of a debt.

Size Distribution of Income

The personal or size distribution of income is a measure of the distribution of national income among individuals/ households. Individuals earn income from employment or other sources such as interest, profit, rent, gifts and inheritances. Size distribution of income is obtained by dividing the population into successive quintiles (or deciles) according to ascending income levels and then determining what proportion of national income is received by each income group.

Skewness

As a statistical term, skewness measures the degree of asymmetry of a distribution. If the frequency curve of a distribution has a longer tail to the right of the central maximum than to the left, the distribution is said to be skewed to the right (positive skewness). If the reverse is true it is said to be skewed to the left (negative skewness).

Sliding Peg **See Crawling Peg**

Smithsonian Agreement

It was signed in December 1971 by the Group of Ten in the Smithsonian Institution Building. It was hailed by the then US President Richard Nixon as 'the most significant agreement in the history of world'. Under this agreement, the structure of exchange rates was realigned by changing the gold parities of most currencies including dollar. While the gold parity of dollar was reduced, it was raised for other currencies. The net result was the devaluation of dollar by around 7 per cent. However, the Agreement broke down after 14 months when US dollar was devalued again and several major currencies began to float.

Social Cost **See Cost of Production**

Social Cost-Benefit Analysis

A private firm typically invests according to commercial profitability. However, national profitability (or social profitability) may differ from commercial profitability. Social cost-benefit analysis is a technique of public project evaluation in order to allocate resources in a way most profitable to society.

The case for social cost-benefit analysis rests on the limitations of commercial or financial profitability analysis. Social cost-benefit analysis, concerned with the appraisal of publicly financed investment projects, answers the question whether resource allocation is profitable to society or not. Contrarily, commercial profitability analysis, concerned with the appraisal of privately-financed projects, examines whether resource allocation is profitable to the entrepreneur or not.

Under commercial profitability approach, private profit is defined as the difference between value of earnings and value of costs. If this is positive, it means there is profit. If it is negative, there is loss. Thus, a private project is profitable if the private benefits of the project exceed private costs.

Social cost-benefit analysis is applied welfare economics in a world of the second-best. In theory, a first-best economy must fulfil the marginal conditions of perfectly competitive product and factor markets. The perfectly competitive solution to resource allocation would then be equivalent to a Pareto-efficient allocation. In reality, investment resources are not allocated in a first-best world of perfect competition. Instances of market failure and distortions are widespread, especially in LDCs. These distortions are commonly in the form of monopolies/oligopolies, taxes, subsidies, tariffs etc. In correcting for these distortions, the practice of project appraisal is an exercise in the theory of the second-best. The price distortions are corrected through shadow pricing, using a cost-benefit analysis based on imputed values.

Externalities do not enter the calculations of private profit. A private industrial project may give rise to air pollution, water pollution (external diseconomies) and other socially undesirable effects. However, private profits based on market valuation do not reflect these. The cost of bad health or unpleasant life does not figure in commercial profits. Since externalities matter so much for social welfare, the choice of public projects must take into account the issue of externalities.

Measuring Social Cost-Benefit (Shadow Prices): Shadow prices (true cost or opportunity cost) of factors constitute the core of social cost-benefit analysis. If employing people in a public project implies reduction in employment and output elsewhere, then social cost of labour is equal to output lost elsewhere. Apparently, the social cost of unemployed labour is zero. Likewise, we can find out the social cost of capital, foreign exchange and other resources.

The rule for measuring social benefit is as follows: the marginal utility that people place on a non-market item is inferred from the money they would have to pay for a market item which they value equally.

Now, if social valuation of cost and benefit is done in terms of shadow prices, we can say that a public project will be profitable to society if the social benefits exceed the social cost.

In measuring social costs and benefits of public projects, the following rules must be followed:

1. Only real costs and benefits should be included and pecuniary (monetary) costs and benefits should be excluded.
2. Both direct and indirect cost and benefits should be taken into account.
3. Valuation of intangible benefits and costs is more difficult. Cost-effectiveness analysis may have to be applied.
4. Shadow pricing corrects the distortions introduced by monopoly, taxes, subsidies etc. These distortions are more widespread in LDCs.
5. In selecting the particular projects to be undertaken allowance must be made for the fact that multiple objectives may be involved.

Social Goods

These are goods the consumption of which is nonrival. They have common utility for the citizens as, for example, services of defence forces and benefits of anti-pollution measures.

Socialism

It is an economic system under which means of production of a country are owned by the state, i.e. all land, buildings, factories, machines and equipments are the property of the government. A socialist or a centrally planned economy is totally different from a capitalist economy.

Movement for socialism began soon after the evolution of capitalism and industrialisation in Western Europe. Socialistic ideas were pioneered by Robert Owen (1771-1858) in Britain in the 19th century. He emphasised removal of poverty without going into the cause of it. French socialists advocated state intervention for the removal of poverty and exploitation. Marxists regard these socialists as utopians.

It was German philosopher Karl Marx (1818-1883) who made a systematic study of the functioning of a capitalist society and predicted its inevitable destruction due to its internal contradictions. The Marxian analysis is based on historical and dialectical materialism. It is also called scientific socialism. However, Marx and his friend Friedrich Engels (1820-1895) concentrated on the weaknesses of the capitalist system and did not say much as to how a socialist system would function. This job was left to Vladimir Lenin (1870-1924), Josif Stalin (1879-1953) and Mao Tse Tung (1893-1976).

A socialist society has certain distinguishing features which make its functioning different from a capitalist society. The nature of an economic system and its functioning depends upon the pattern of ownership of the means of production. Socialism is an economic system characterised by state ownership of the means of production.

Some means of production may be owned by co-operatives and private individuals. However, private sector is prohibited from employing wage labour. Private sector production is permitted if it employs family labour. Thus, small-scale production is allowed to exist in a socialist system.

Socialism necessarily implies that the means of production are used for the benefit of society as a whole. Socialism implies a change both in the ownership of the means of production and the motivation of this ownership.

Social ownership of the means of production eliminates classes in the system which are antagonistic to each other. Socialist production is a non-antagonistic mode of production. The source of conflict, viz. private property does not exist and therefore class conflict is absent in a socialist system. However, certain types of class conflict may continue to exist as, for example, between bureaucrats and workers, rural sector and urban sector, intellectuals and non-intellectuals and blue collar and white collar workers.

In a socialist society, wage labour of the capitalist system does not exist. The institution of wage labour involves the divorce of the worker from the ownership and management of the means of production. Under socialism, the worker is the owner of the means of production and the production process is managed by the workers.

Planning is a Central Feature of Socialism: Decisions regarding production and distribution are centrally taken. However, some degree of freedom may be allowed to production units.

The role of market mechanism is limited. Market exists for consumer goods and labour but there is no market for capital goods. In the consumer goods market, the supply of consumer goods is determined by the state. Consumer sovereignty of the capitalist society is non-existent under socialism because supply is state determined. However, the consumer is free in his demand behaviour. In the labour market, the state determines the employment availability. The workers are free to choose between the available jobs.

Equitable distribution of economic power is another feature of socialism. Strictly speaking, it is an effect rather than a feature of socialism. Some inequalities continue to exist but these inequalities are necessary as incentives for harder work. Inequalities of unearned incomes are absent because of socialisation of property. Inequalities of income arising out of work are allowed to exist in limited degree.

Allocation of Resources: The possibility and practicability of rational allocation of resources in a socialist economy has been a subject of great controversy among economists. Since both the supply and demand for capital are determined by the state, there is no market for capital goods. This fact has raised the controversy, first about the theoretical possibility, and second about the practicability of efficient allocation of resources in a socialist economy.

Though market exists for consumer goods and labour, its scope is limited. Thus, in the consumer goods market, the supply is pre-determined by the state and the consumer has the freedom to buy or not to buy. In the labour market, the state determines the demand for labour and the labourer is free to choose between available occupations.

According to German economist Ludwig Von Mises, there is no market and hence no market prices for capital goods in a socialist economy. Prices of capital goods would, therefore, be determined arbitrarily. Thus, resource allocation would be arbitrary and not rational. He claimed that economic calculation is impossible in a socialist society. By formulating this central problem of a socialist economy, he posed a challenge to the socialist economists. The challenge was ably met by Fred Taylor and Oscar Lange.

Fred Tylor in a paper published in 1929 indicated how a socialist economy would solve the problem by a method of trial and error. This method was further elucidated by Oscar Lange.

Lange starts by reviewing the three conditions required for economic equilibrium in a competitive market. These are: (a) subjective conditions, (b) objective conditions and (c) macro conditions.

The subjective conditions relate to the individual consumers and producers. The subjective conditions are satisfied where producers and consumers attain maximum benefit positions. The objective conditions relate to equilibrium of the industry. The objective conditions are satisfied when demand equals supply for each commodity. The price at which demand equals supply will be an equilibrium price only if this price ensures simultaneously the subjective conditions. The macro-equilibrium refers to the equilibrium of the social organisation of the economic system. This requires that the level of national income and the pattern of income distribution are consistent. The three equilibrium conditions are inter-dependent.

According to Lange, equilibrium in a socialist society can be achieved by a method of trial and error similar to that in a competitive economy.

Let the central planning board start with a given set of prices chosen at random. All decisions of the managers of production (state officials) and of individuals as consumers and as suppliers of labour are made on the basis of these prices. As a result of these decisions, the quantity demanded and supplied of each commodity is determined.

If the quantity demanded of a commodity is not equal to the quantity supplied, the price of that commodity has to be changed. It has to be raised if demand exceeds supply and lowered if the reverse is the case. Thus, the central planning board fixes a new set of prices which serves as a basis for new decisions. The new set of decisions results in a new set of quantities demanded and supplied. Through this process of trial and error, equilibrium prices are finally determined.

Actually, the process of trial and error would proceed on the basis of the prices historically given. Relatively small adjustments of those prices would constantly be required. There would be no necessity of building up an entirely new price system at random basis. Thus, the accounting prices in a socialist economy can be determined by the same process of trial and error by which prices in a competitive market are determined.

In fact, the socialist economists have claimed that trial and error procedure works much better in a socialist economy than it does in a competitive market. In other words, resource allocation is much more efficient under socialism. The reason is that the trial and error process is likely to be shorter in a socialist economy. If this is so the waste occurring during the adjustment process will be smaller.

The trial and error process is likely to be shorter in a socialist economy because the central planning board has a much wider knowledge of what is going on in the whole economy than any private entrepreneur can ever have. It can quickly arrive at the equilibrium prices on the basis of historically determined prices. Thus, Lange opined that economic accounting is not only possible and practicable but also more efficient in a socialist economy as compared to a capitalist economy.

Incentives in a Socialist Society : Labour is an active factor of production. It needs incentives to work harder and for longer hours. Economic and non-economic incentives ensure fulfilment of production targets and other objectives.

In a capitalist economy means of production are owned by individuals who use them for maximising profits. The guide to maximisation of private welfare is the price mechanism. With the help of prices of commodities and factors of production, the individual entrepreneurs take production decisions keeping in mind the objective function (i.e. profit maximisation). Private profit is, thus, the measure of performance as well as the source of incentives. In fact, private profit is the driving force of capitalism.

The structure of a socialist economy is fundamentally different from that of a capitalist economy. Under socialism, means of production are owned by the state. Production and all economic activities are carried on for the satisfaction of the needs of the society. The basic mode of economic activity is through planning i.e. productive economic process is consciously and purposively guided by state agencies.

In a socialist economy, price mechanism does not have the same influence in guiding economic decisions as it has in a capitalist economy. Moreover, success is no longer measured in terms of maximisation of individual or private welfare. In fact, a socialist system emphasises social objectives and maximisation of society's welfare. Consequently, success indicators are furnished by the state or the central planning board in terms of physical output or value of output. The success indicators reflect the efficiency of the economic system in general and the enterprise and factors of production in particular. They measure the extent to which plans are fulfilled.

It is recognised that even a socialist system cannot do without a system of incentives if plan targets are to be fulfilled. These incentives are based on the success indicators.

The problem of incentives in a socialist economy is essentially the problem of compromising between social objectives and encouragement to individual factor owners. This contradiction does not arise in the capitalist system where the objectives are private and incentives are individual-based. In the socialist system, however, an individual-based system of incentives contradicts the spirit of socialism. The attempt in a socialist system, therefore, is to minimise the dependence on individual incentives and to encourage collective incentives.

Broadly speaking, incentives in a socialist economy can be classified into two categories: (a) economic incentives and (b) social incentives (social status).

This classification is not valid in a capitalist society where social status, to a large extent, is a function of one's economic status. In a socialist system, however, it is possible to separate one's economic status from one's social status.

Economic incentives include incentives in the form of wages, community welfare benefits, holidays etc. Social incentives relate to one's position in society as, for example, membership of various committees and boards, and being in a socially honoured list. The attempt to minimise capitalist values is interpreted to mean a shift from economic to social incentives.

Soft Currency See Currency

Soft-to-Tax Incomes

In every country, there are some soft-to-tax incomes as against certain Hard-to-Tax Incomes (q.v.). Wages and salaries are properly recorded and therefore it is easy to assess and collect taxes on them through the Pay-As-You-Earn (q.v.) system. Similarly, income from securities paid through banks can easily be subjected to deduction of tax at source.

Source Rule of Foreign Income See Double Taxation

Source Theory of Income

Among the various indices of ability-to-pay taxes, income is regarded by far the most appropriate. This is borne out by the popularity of income taxes the world over. Though widely accepted as the appropriate base for taxation, the concept of income is nebulous. To operate an income tax system, it is necessary to define as to what constitutes *income*. In spite of the voluminous literature on the subject, there is no universally accepted single definition of income.

Traditionally, income is defined in terms of two alternative approaches: (a) source theory of income and (b) Net Accretion Theory of Income (q.v.). According to source theory, defended by Adolf Wagner among others, only those receipts should form part of taxable income which arise from a permanent source and therefore ensure regular flow of the receipts. Thus, non-recurrent receipts such as lottery prizes, gifts received and capital gains should be excluded from the taxable base. Since irregular incomes are substantial in modern economies and reflect an enhanced ability-to-pay on the part of recipients, source theory has few takers and it is as good as discarded.

South Asian Association for Regional Co-operation (SAARC)

On December 8, 1985, the seven South Asian States, viz. India, Pakistan, Nepal, Bangladesh, Bhutan, Sri Lanka, and Maldives formally launched the South Asian Association for Regional Cooperation (SAARC). Broadly speaking, SAARC countries comprise the Indian sub-continent, an area which was usually referred to, prior to 1947, as Britain's Indian empire. Sharing a common colonial legacy of socio-economic backwardness, they inhabit one-fifth of world population and face the twin formidable problems of unemployment and poverty. At the same time, these countries provide a vast investment and market potential in a basically free enterprise environment. SAARC, with its headquarters located in Kathmandu, Nepal, is an example of south-south co-operation.

The underlying objective of this regional grouping is to strive for co-operative efforts to accelerate the economic development of this region, one of the poorest in the world. This institutional arrangement is intended to provide scope for discussing bilateral issues and exploring areas for co-operative linkages in socio-economic field. SAARC charter pledges non-interference by members in each others internal affairs. Under its rules, all decisions are to be unanimous and no tendentious issues can be brought before this forum. This is one hope for the smooth and expanding co-operation among the member countries despite their different systems of governance. Areas identified for mutual co-operation range from agriculture, forestry, health and population, science and technology, art and culture and curbing terrorism.

Spatial Externalities **See Spill-overs**

Special Drawing Rights (SDRs)

These were created as a new and additional form of international reserves/liquidity in 1970 under the International Monetary Fund (IMF). Under this scheme, countries receive SDRs as per their share in reserve assets and have an automatic right to draw them from IMF over and above other drawing facilities. SDRs constitute a permanent net addition to international liquidity.

A deficit country uses SDRs for settling deficit by exchanging SDRs for whatever currency it requires. Other countries accept SDRs as gold or convertible currencies. Its value is based on the values of a *standard basket* of five major currencies. Thus, SDRs are like monetary gold or assets that have no corresponding liability. In balance of payments, allocation of SDRs (credit) forms the counterpart that matches the rise (debit) in a country's holding of SDRs which form the part of reserves. Most central banks include SDRs as assets.

It was in 1967 that the Board of Governors of the IMF agreed at the annual meetings in Rio de Janeiro to create a new international monetary reserve asset to be named the special drawing right. SDRs can be created only by the IMF. The legal framework for their creation and allocation to member countries was established by the first amendment to the Articles of Agreement of the IMF adopted in 1968. The second amendment (1978) provided for a considerable liberalisation of the rules governing the use of the SDRs. On

January 1, 1970, the first distribution of 3.4 billion SDRs was made to IMF member countries followed by subsequent distributions.

Special Economic Zones (SEZs)

SEZs in a country are exempt from rules and regulations governing exports and imports. The entire production has to be exported from these zones. SEZs are treated as if they are outside the customs territory of the country. The units are able to import capital goods and raw materials duty free. The movement of goods to and from SEZs is unrestricted. There is generally a fiscal incentive package (including tax holiday) for export units located in SEZs.

It is noteworthy that SEZs have played a crucial role in boosting China's exports and presently the country derives 40 per cent of its exports from such zones. Chinese SEZs are based on contract labour system (hire and fire policy).

Specific Duty

A specific or volumetric duty represents a fixed amount of tax on a unit of the physical quantity of the product. Customs duties, excise levies and sales taxes on commodities may take specific or *ad valorem* form.

Specific duty is generally preferred for commodities the classifications and sub-classifications of which are not numerous, i.e. the commodity is a standardised one, e.g. sugar. A specific duty is easy to apply besides having the political and psychological advantages of obscuring the actual ratio of the tax to the selling price. However, it is price-neutral in the sense that price changes in the commodity do not affect the revenue yield. Specific duty is quality-neutral also unless differential rates are prescribed with reference to the quality of the product.

There can be many variants of the specific form of duty. If a flat amount per unit of a commodity is levied irrespective of the price range, it is a simple specific duty. It may be simple specific with initial exemption. However, if the flat amount per unit changes with the price range of the commodity, it becomes a graduated specific duty. See also *Ad Valorem* Duty; and Compound Duty.

Spill-overs

Spill-overs (or spatial externalities) occur where the benefits of a locally provided service spread to persons who are not legally required to contribute to the cost of the service. Services the benefits of which generally spill over to neighbouring jurisdictions include public transport, subsidised educational and medical facilities, anti-pollution measures, parks and recreational facilities

Spite Effect

This term, attributed to Richard Musgrave, means individuals may work less as a result of a tax increase in order to take revenge on the government. People become resentful and are willing to deprive themselves if they can also see that they are simultaneously depriving the tax authorities.

Split Rate System

Under this system, profits distributed as dividends are taxed at a lower rate than retained earnings (i.e. undistributed profits). See also Corporate Income Tax.

Splitting Method

Under it, tax liability of husband and wife is determined amounting to twice the tax due on half of their combined income. For example, if husband and wife each earn a taxable income of Rs. 80,000 and Rs. 60,000 respectively, the joint tax liability would be twice the tax on Rs. 70,000. See also Quotient Method; and Tax Treatment of Family Income.

Spot Deal

It is a deal for a currency for delivery within two business days. It is also known as value spot.

Spot Exchange Rate See Exchange Rate

Spot Market See Forward and Spot Markets

Spread

It is the difference between the buying and selling prices of a currency.

Square Position

When sales and purchases of a currency are equal, it is known as a square position. It is also called s*quare book, flat book* or *matched book*.

STABEX Compensatory Finance Scheme See Lome Treaty

Stable and Unstable Equilibrium

Market equilibrium is determined by forces of demand and supply. If price changes, the producers want to sell a different quantity. In most cases, it is not possible for the producers to quickly adjust their supply to price changes. In other words, there is a lag between the decision to change quantity supplied and the actual change in it. This phenomenon is called *supply lag*. A good example of supply lag is the time interval between successive agricultural crops. A farmer looks at current year's price while deciding what crop to grow next year. Similarly, current year's supply depends on last year's price.

An equilibrium condition is stable if any deviation from the equilibrium brings into operation market forces which restore back the equilibrium.

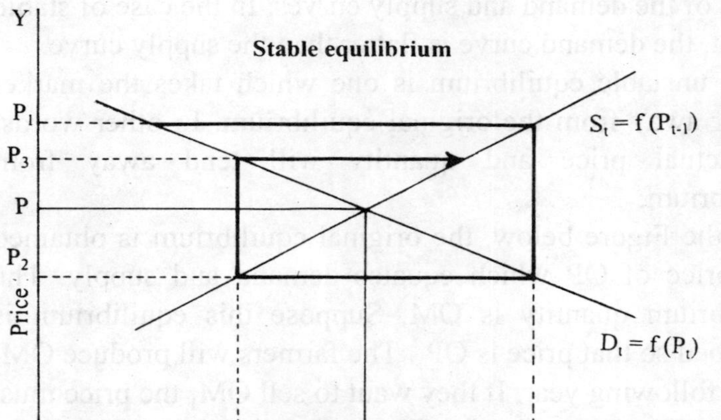

In the Figure above, the original equilibrium is achieved at a price of OP which equates demand and supply. The equilibrium quantity is OM. Suppose this equilibrium is disturbed so that the price is OP_1. The farmers will produce OM_1 in the following year. If they want to sell OM_1 the price must fall to OP_2. The price at OP_2 will induce the farmers to produce OM_2. When this quantity comes to the market in the following year, the price will rise to OP_3. Repeating the whole process it is clear that the price and quantity will oscillate around the original equilibrium in a series of diminishing fluctuations. If nothing further disturbs the market, the price and quantity will eventually approach the original equilibrium. This is a case of stable adjustment mechanism.

What makes it stable equilibrium? The difference between stable and unstable markets lies in the relative slopes of the demand and supply curves. In the case of stable market, the demand curve is flatter than the supply curve.

An unstable equilibrium is one which takes the market further away from the original equilibrium. In other words, the actual price and quantity will tend away from equilibrium.

In the Figure below, the original equilibrium is obtained at a price of OP which equates demand and supply. The equilibrium quantity is OM. Suppose this equilibrium is disturbed so that price is OP_1. The farmers will produce OM_1 in the following year. If they want to sell OM_1 the price must fall to OP_2. The price at OP_2 will induce the farmers to produce OM_2. When this quantity reaches the market in the following year, the price will rise to OP_3. Repeating the whole process, it is found that the price and quantity move away from the equilibrium point. This is a case of unstable adjustment mechanism.

What makes it unstable? It is the relative slopes of the demand and supply curves. In the case of unstable equilibrium, the supply curve is flatter than the demand curve.

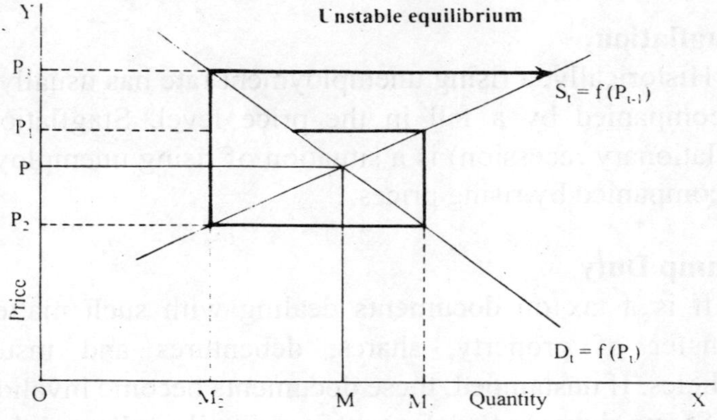

Stages of Tax Structure Development

Like civilisations, tax systems evolve over centuries. Harley Hinrichs in his book *General Theory of Tax Structure Change During Economic Development* has mentioned five stages through which tax structure has changed historically as economies have developed. These are: First Stage: A traditional society relies primarily on traditional direct taxes like taxes on land, livestock, water rights etc. Second Stage: Society breaks away from old ways and indirect taxes become more important, especially external indirect taxes (i.e. taxes on foreign trade). Third Stage: Traditional direct taxes decline relative to national income and governmental revenues. Fourth Stage: Domestic commodity production increases and internal indirect taxes (excise duties and sales taxes) grow rapidly to replace customs duties. Fifth Stage: Economy gains maturity and modern direct taxes like personal income and corporate profit taxes become dominant.

Stagflation

Historically, a rising unemployment rate has usually been accompanied by a fall in the price level. Stagflation (or inflationary recession) is a situation of rising unemployment accompanied by rising prices.

Stamp Duty

It is a tax on documents dealing with such matters as transfer of property, shares, debentures and insurance policies. If unstamped, these documents become invalid.

Stamp duty (or transfer tax) is generally collected through the sale of revenue stamps which must be affixed or imprinted on the document in question. Stamp duties are often under the jurisdiction of state and local governments.

Standard Deduction

It is common in the income tax laws of countries to allow deduction of expenditures from gross salary income incurred by taxpayers for employment purposes. If the deduction is allowed only on production or proof of having incurred such expenditure, the procedure will obviously be cumbersome for salaried persons. To simplify rules, many countries allow a standard deduction, from aggregate amount of salary, for all types of expenditure incurred towards employment. For example, in India, the standard deduction allowed for the financial year 1999-2000 is Rs. 20,000. Standard deduction is allowed to an employee irrespective of his designation and regardless of the fact whether any expenditure incidental to employment has actually been incurred or not by him.

Standard Deviation

Standard deviation is the square root of variance. Variance is the average of squared deviations about the arithmetic mean.

Standard International Trade Classification (SITC)

This classification is meant to simplify reference to thousands of commodities traded world-wide. Each commodity has a special number attached to it which is acceptable among all those countries adopting SITC. This classification starts from a single digit broad section referring to the nature of the commodity and then it is divided into divisions and groups. At present, WTO/UNCTAD use SITC (3rd Revision). The following nine sections signify the nature of the commodity:

0 Food and live animals
1 Beverages and tobacco
2 Crude materials, inedible, except fuels
3 Mineral fuels, lubricants and related materials
4 Animal and vegetable oils and fats
5 Chemicals
6 Manufactured goods classified chiefly by materials
7 Machinery and transport equipment
8 Miscellaneous manufactured articles
9 Commodities not classified according to kind.

Statistics

Statistics as a subject deals with scientific methods for collecting, organising, summarising, presenting and analysing data to draw valid conclusions and take decisions on the basis of such conclusions. In a plural sense, the term is used to denote the data themselves as, for example, rainfall statistics and export and import statistics.

Stochastic Variable **See Variable**

Stock Market

A stock (or share) market deals mainly in corporate securities like shares and debentures. The purpose of these securities is to raise long-term funds for companies engaged in production. Thus, stock market is an important component of the capital market of the financial system.

Function of the stock market is two-fold: (a) to arrange for the raising of new capital (primary market function) and (b) to provide liquidity to existing securities (secondary market function).

New capital is raised by the issue of shares and debentures. Corporate enterprises raising new capital may be new companies or existing companies planning expansion of their operations. Sometimes, existing private firms *go public*, i.e. become public limited companies.

Stock market helps the floatation of new issue by providing a variety of services like underwriting, distribution and listing of the issue. Underwriting means guaranteeing the purchase of a fixed amount of new issue by the underwriter. The new issue of capital may be a public issue or a right issue or both in certain proportions. It may be in the form of equity shares or debentures. Debentures, in turn, may be fully convertible, partly convertible or non-convertible into shares. A public issue means the general public is invited to subscribe to the new issue. A right issue is restricted for subscription by existing shareholders of the company.

Stock exchanges provide facilities for secondary market, i.e. transactions in existing securities. People desirous of converting their cash into securities can go to the stock exchange and buy securities through brokers. Similarly, securities can be converted into cash by selling them in the market. Transactions in the secondary market reflect investment climate in the economy.

Stocks and Flows

Both stocks and flows are variables or quantities. Flows have time dimension, i.e. they are measured over a period of time. Conversely, stocks are measured at a particular point of time. Like a balance sheet, a stock position has a reference to a particular date and shows position on that date. A flow shows change during a period of time.

Thus, national income is a flow variable because it describes and measures the flow of goods and services which become available to a country during a year. Contrarily, national capital is a stock variable which shows, on a particular date, the stock of machines, plants, buildings etc. owned by a country.

In short, all economic variables which are related to a period of time are called flow variables, e.g. income, expenditure, savings, depreciation and change in inventories. Conversely, all economic variables which are related to a point of time are known as stock variables, e.g. capital, wealth and foreign debt. Stock and flow variables are interrelated. Thus, increase in national income increases national capital and increase in national capital generates larger national income.

Straight Line Depreciation Method

Under this method, the historic cost of the depreciating asset is apportioned in equal amounts for deduction over the period of its estimated economic life which is normally specified in the tax law for each group of assets. Thus, if a machine is purchased for Rs. 50,000 and the tax law specifies that this asset can be written off at a rate of 20 per cent, then the yearly depreciation deduction will be Rs. 10,000 for 5 years. See also Declining-Balance Depreciation Method.

Structural Unemployment See Unemployment

Subsidy

A subsidy is a grant of money from an outside third party to either the buyer or the seller of a commodity. Subsidies allow a buyer to procure a commodity/service at a lower price than would otherwise have been necessary. The effect of a subsidy is opposite of the effect of a tax.

A business firm will not stay in operation unless revenue is sufficient enough to cover cost plus some return on investment. If revenue from buyers is insufficient, a subsidy from an outside agency may keep the firm in operation.

Subsistence Farming

As against the commercialised nature of agricultural operations in the developed countries, farming in less developed countries still remains a source of livelihood for most farmers. The main reason for this is the low per capita availability of land. Moreover, productivity is low because of traditional agricultural practices.

Subsistence Theory of Wages See Wages

Succession Duty See Inheritance Tax

Sumptuary Tax

It is a kind of excise on goods generally thought to have socially harmful effects. The best examples of such goods are alcoholic beverages and cigarettes. High taxes on these luxury items are imposed with a view to discourage their consumption and also on the ground that those who buy them can afford to pay additional tax.

Supply

Like demand, the concept of supply has a special meaning in economics. Supply means the quantity of a commodity which an individual producer is willing to supply over a specific time period and at a specific price. Supply of a commodity is determined by a host of factors including price of the commodity, production technology and cost of inputs. Change in technology influences a firm's supply function by altering the cost of production. Use of more efficient and automatic equipment may lower cost, enabling a firm to offer more supply at the same price. Another non-price factor influencing supply is the availability and cost of inputs used in the production process. If the cost of labour (wages) increases, supply will decrease if price remains the same. Sometimes supply of a commodity is also influenced by the prices of related commodities. For example, a decrease in the price of wheat may induce farmers to switch over to rice cultivation. Thus, the supply of rice will increase although no change has occurred in its price.

Other things being equal, as price of a commodity increases, the quantity supplied also increases, and as price decreases the quantity supplied also decreases. Or, the supply of a commodity is positively or directly related to its price. This is called the law of supply. It is simple logic that firms are encouraged to supply more of sugar at higher prices because they expect to earn larger profits. Contrarily, less sugar will be offered for sale at lower prices because profit margin declines.

Supply Lag **See Stable and Unstable Equilibrium**

Surcharge

It is an additional tax calculated on the normal tax liability. In other words, surcharge is assessed on the usual amount of tax due.

Surtax

An additional tax levied on a tax base after a normal tax has been applied. Usually, it is applied to income above a certain level to achieve desired progressivity of the rate schedule. For example, if normal corporate income tax is 35 per cent of all net income, an additional surtax of 20 per cent may be imposed on all taxable incomes above a certain amount (say Rs. 50,000). The Excess Profit Tax (q.v.) levied on companies is a surtax, i.e. an extra tax.

Sustainable Development

The concept of sustainable development advocates economic progress in an environmentally responsible manner. Sustainable development attempts to strike a proper balance between the requirements of economic development and the need for the protection of environment. It tries to combine the elements of economic efficiency, intergenerational equity, social concerns and environmental protection. Although, the term sustainable development has many interpretations, it generally refers to non-declining human well-being over time.

Swap Rate

Exchange rate differential between the spot rate and the 3-month forward rate for a currency against another currency is called swap rate.

Swap Transactions

These are transactions in which a currency is bought and sold simultaneously but delivery dates for the purchase and sale are different. Net exchange position remains the same even if there is a change in the spot rate of the currencies.

T

Tangible Asset See Asset

Tariff

It is a tax imposed by authorities on imports with various motives including cut in imports, protection to domestic industries or to earn revenue. Tariff imposed on imported goods according to their value is called *ad valorem* tariff.

Tariff-Quota

It displays both tariff-like and quota-like characteristics. Tariff-quota provides for the entry of a product in a specified quantity at one tariff rate (within quota rate), but imports in excess of that quantity are subject to a higher rate of tariff (over-quota rate). Thus, it is a two-tier tariff. It is generally viewed as a compromise between the interest of the consumers who desire low cost imports, and those of the domestic producers who desire protectionism.

Tariff Schedule

It is a schedule containing tariff rates for imported items on which tariff is imposed.

Tariff Union

It is a group of countries having a common customs legislation imposing tariff for non-members countries and abolition of tariff among themselves.

Tax

A tax is a compulsory payment made to general government without any direct *quid pro quo*. General government includes central, state and local governments. Tax payments are compulsory and the benefits provided by government to taxpayers are neither direct nor proportional to such payments. Every tax is made up of two elements: a base, i.e. the object to be taxed, and a rate structure indicating how the base is to be taxed.

Distinction between tax and non-tax revenue of a government is not watertight. There are some borderline cases which pertain to certain fees and charges levied in connection with a specific service or activity. Sometimes, it is difficult to distinguish between a fee and a tax. For example, vehicle licence fee is generally regarded as a tax.

Definition of a tax given above is subject to modifications in view of the differing practices of tax authorities in different countries. The Organisation for Economic Co-operation and Development considers the following fees and charges as non-tax revenues: court fees, driving licence fees, harbour fees, passport fees, radio and television licence fees where public authorities provide the service. Fines and penalties relating to tax offences are treated as tax revenues whereas fines relating to non-tax offences (e.g. traffic violations) are included in non-tax revenues.

A modern government undertakes welfare and developmental activities and makes provision for public goods to satisfy collective needs of the people. It has also to pay for its own administration. It needs financial resources for these purposes and taxation is one method of transferring money from private to public hands.

Taxation is necessary because what the government gives it must first take away. According to Kalidas, the great Sanskrit poet of ancient India, "Just as the sun extracts water from the reservoirs and gives it back in the form of showers, so does the ruler extract tax from his subjects and gives it back to them in the form of prosperity." See also Tax Policy.

Taxable Capacity

In simple terms, it denotes the extent to which the citizens of a country can be taxed. Determination of the taxable capacity of people is difficult because it depends on a host of factors, including what the government does with the revenue raised through taxes.

Technically, taxable capacity refers to the presumed ability of the government to generate taxes. Its quantitative determination involves the use of cross-sectional data of the explanatory variables of taxable capacity in a regression equation. Taxable capacity is estimated by regressing tax ratio on variables considered to influence taxable capacity.

Taxable capacities differ in different countries. Therefore, as a first step, it is necessary to identify variables which influence taxable capacity. Tax literature mentions a long list of such variables including per capita income, composition of gross domestic product, degree of openness of the economy and so on. Various permutations and combinations of these variables using cross-sectional data are embodied in a regression equation to estimate taxable capacity.

Taxable Entities See Units of Assessment

Taxable Income

It is that part of an assessee's income which is liable to tax. It is arrived at by deducting from assessable income all allowable deductions.

Tax Accounting

It is a branch of accounting dealing with computation of tax liabilities of assessees, preparing tax returns and keeping tax records for them. Tax accountants are often employed by business concerns to advise them on how to minimise tax liability and to guide them regarding tax implications of business decisions.

Tax Allowance

A tax allowance is used to reduce the taxable income of a firm through exemptions and deductions. It is different from a Tax Credit (q.v.) which directly reduces the amount of tax to be paid.

Tax Amnesty

It refers to an opportunity offered by a government to tax evaders to declare their past concealment of income, wealth etc., without fear of being prosecuted. Tax amnesty (or impunity) is granted only for the past in order to secure better compliance and higher tax yield in the present and future.

A tax amnesty brings concealed money in the open, broadens the base of investment and hence accelerates economic development.

However, tax amnesties set bad precedents and encourage tax evaders in the hope that they will be let off leniently for their past sins any time in the future. Practically, the same group of tax evaders takes advantage of tax amnesties announced by a government. Honest taxpayers are demoralised and tax enforcement machinery also loses respect in the eyes of the common man.

Tax Anticipation Bills

These are short-term, interest-bearing credit instruments sold by the United States Treasury to business firms which may use them to pay taxes. Treasury tax anticipation bills are sold at auctions, at a discount, and mature when taxes are due. Business firms have the advantage of earning interest while the government receives tax revenue at regular intervals and in a more even flow.

Tax Avoidance

It means preventing or reducing one's tax liability through manipulations within the framework of existing tax legislation. Tax avoidance, as against Tax Evasion (q.v.), is legally permissible and hence a legitimate aim of taxpayers.

Tax avoidance is attempted through such devices as formation of holding companies to claim artificial deductions, constitution of trusts and family partnerships, transfer of income earning assets to one's wife and children for fractioning income for tax purposes, investing in provident funds and life insurance policies, and manipulation of capital gains.

Since tax avoidance has a colour of legality about it, clever taxpayers do their best to avoid or keep down tax payments. This may force the government to raise tax rates, making the less clever assessees bear a disproportionate tax burden.

Tax laws in many countries incorporate anti-tax avoidance provisions under which certain incomes are included in an assessee's total income, though such incomes legally belong to other persons.

In India, Sections 60 to 65 of the Income Tax Act, 1961, deal with instances where an assessee may attempt to reduce his tax liability either by transferring his assets in favour of his family members or by arranging his sources of income in such a manner that tax incidence falls on others whereas benefit of income, directly or indirectly, is derived by the assessee himself. Thus, incomes arising to the spouse, minor child, son's wife, son's minor child and certain other persons are clubbed with the assessee's income in certain circumstances.

Tax Base

Base of a tax is the legal description of the object which is taxed. Tax bases, or what Richard Musgrave calls *tax handles*, are numerous but the following are common ones. Base of excise duty is the value/quantity of a commodity; of sales tax, the sales of business; of customs duty, the crossing of goods over national frontiers; of inter-state sales tax, the crossing of goods over boundaries of states within a country; of octroi/terminal taxes, the crossing of goods over boundaries of local areas within a state; of income tax, the income earned by corporate and non-corporate assessees during an accounting year; of gift tax, the value of gifts made by an assessee during an accounting year.

Broadening the tax base means application of a tax to a larger portion of the object already being taxed. Erosion of the tax base means narrowing of the tax base through special exemptions and concessions. A good tax base is one which can easily be measured and monitored. Thus, a realised capital gain is a good base for taxation as compared to an accrued capital gain.

It is the availability of tax bases that determines the nature of tax system in a country. Furthermore, it is the nature of the tax base that determines the final resting place of the burden of a tax. To quote Richard Musgrave, "Apart from the level and distribution of income, the availability of 'tax handles' is related to the economic structure of the country. Thus, the administration of an income tax is much more difficult where employment is in small establishments. Profits taxation is not feasible until accounting practices attain minimal standards, and it is difficult if firms are small and unstable. Product taxes cannot be imposed at the retail level if retail establishments are small and impermanent. Effective land taxation is difficult where food is home-consumed, the agricultural sector is largely non-monetised, and land surveys are inadequate in providing proper valuations. On the other hand, taxation is simplified in a highly open economy where imports and exports pass through major ports and thus can be readily established by tax authorities."

A closed economy will have no customs revenue and an agricultural economy with small business establishments cannot operate corporation tax. The relative importance of various tax bases differs in different countries and it may change in a country over a period of time.

Tax Credit

Tax credit (or tax rebate) is a legal provision permitting taxpayers to deduct specified sums from their tax liability. A tax credit differs from a deduction because the former is subtracted after the total tax liability has been calculated whereas the latter is subtracted from the income subject to tax.

Apparently, a tax credit of a given amount is more valuable to a taxpayer than a deduction of the same amount. For example, a taxpayer who is in the 40 per cent bracket of individual income tax reduces his total burden by Rs. 1,000 if he is allowed a tax credit of Rs. 1,000. However, his tax burden is reduced by Rs. 400 if he is given a deduction of Rs. 1,000.

Tax Deduction at Source **See Withholding Tax**

Tax Effort

Actual tax ratio when divided by the computed tax ratio (taxable capacity) gives the index of tax effort. If the resulting value is greater than unity, it indicates a relatively high tax effort or performance and vice versa. Thus, tax effort defines the extent to which a country uses its Taxable Capacity (q.v.).

Computation of a tax effort index permits inter-country comparisons. For example, if country A's level of taxation is below the sample average, it means it is making low tax efforts. Since taxable capacity factors have already been taken into account, the explanation for low tax efforts is to be sought in non-economic factors like resistance of vested interests against higher taxes or lack of political will to tax certain sectors of the economy, e.g. agricultural sector.

Tax Equity

It refers to *fair* or *just* or *equitable* distribution of tax burden among taxpayers. Though fairness and justness in taxation are universally accepted, these terms are rarely defined rigorously and can be interpreted in various ways. Hence, there is no unanimity of opinion as to the type of tax system which results in the most equitable distribution of tax burden.

There are two main approaches to tax equity in tax literature: the Benefit Principle of Taxation (q.v.) which states that tax payments should be proportional to the benefits derived from government services, and the Ability-to-Pay Principle of Taxation (q.v.) which holds that each taxpayer should contribute to the public exchequer in line with his ability-to-pay.

Issues of equity and justice in designing taxes are complex because the notion of justice varies from society to society and from individual to individual. Hence, the notion of tax equity is an undefinable ideal.

Tax Evasion

It is an illegal attempt to reduce tax payable through deliberate under-reporting/non-reporting taxable incomes or concealing one's true *state of affairs* from tax authorities. Tax evasion is a criminal offence and if detected is punishable by financial penalties or even by imprisonment or both.

The following devices are generally employed to evade income tax: 1. Non-reporting/under-reporting of taxable income. 2. Making fraudulent changes in account books. 3. Maintaining multiple set of account books. 4. Keeping transactions out of account books. 5. Opening and operating bank accounts under assumed names. 6. Doing business in the name of dummies. 7. Over-reporting expenses. 8.

Fragmenting income to reduce tax liability. 9. Transfer pricing manipulations (by companies).

Although evasion of tax is a common tendency among people belonging to different groups, opportunities for it vary according to the nature of income earned by taxpayers. In the case of income from salaries and interest from deposits, evasion is less likely because of proper recording and auditing of transactions, and deduction of tax at source. However, opportunities for tax evasion are ample in the case of self-employed in businesses and professions. Doctors, lawyers, architects, property dealers, individual contractors can evade taxes more easily than others. They can insist on their customers to pay them in cash or accept invoices which underestimate the payment.

Causes of Tax Evasion: Among the host of causes of tax evasion, the level of tax rates is probably the most crucial. It is widely believed that higher the rate of tax, the greater is the tendency to evade taxes. High tax rates make tax evasion more tempting. Tax evaders readily take risk if they know that in the event of success the reward is high.

Tax evasion is more in countries where people show apathy towards the government and its laws. People will have less respect for tax laws if they perceive the tax system to be unfair, i.e. the level of taxation (tax-GDP ratio) is high and/or distribution of tax burden among various classes is iniquitous. Salaried persons envy tax evasion opportunities available to self-employed professionals and retail traders, and are tempted to conceal their incomes from non-salary sources. Similarly, taxpayers may feel that government is indulging in wasteful expenditure, e.g. digging the roads too often or spending excessively on government functionaries.

Lenient penal action in case violation of law is detected also encourages tax evasion. Tax evasion by politicians and bureaucrats sends wrong signals to the general public that non-compliance is acceptable. A regime of controls, licences, and shortages also breeds tax evasion and black money.

The problem of tax evasion in underdeveloped countries is associated with the peculiar characteristics of their economies which, in most cases, are agriculture-based in the sense that a substantial part of national income originates from and the majority of the work force is engaged in agriculture. Moreover, there is widespread illiteracy, lack of accounting practices, limited monetisation, and shortage of administrative resources.

Consequences of Tax Evasion: The economy of a country suffers badly as a result of widespread tax evasion.

1. Tax evasion cuts at the very root of the revenue potential of a tax system and therefore hinders the resource mobilisation efforts of a government. Lack of funds may distort implementation of development plans and force the government to resort to deficit financing in case public expenditure is inelastic.

2. Tax evasion may interfere with the declared economic policies of a government by distorting saving and investment patterns and influencing the availability of resources to various sectors of the economy. For instance, a government may impose credit restrictions to discourage certain activities (e.g. speculation) but money saved through tax evasion may be used to finance and encourage the same activities.

3. Tax evasion seriously undermines the equity attribute of a tax system. Honest taxpayers, who are obliged to bear

disproportionate tax burdens, feel demoralised and are tempted to join the tax evaders' camp.

4. Tax evasion leads to the creation of Black Money (q.v.) which in turn is a menace to the economy in its own way. Tax evasion and black money result into concentration of economic power in the hands of undesirable groups in the country.

5. Tax evasion eats into the time and energy of the tax administration which is forced to unravel the intricate ways of tax dodgers.

6. Tax evasion leads to degradation of social and moral standards. Social abuses like bribes, intimidation, blackmailing, tampering with official records, submitting fake documents etc., all go with tax evasion.

Measures to Curb Tax Evasion: The following methods may be adopted by governments to check tax evasion: (a) lowering of tax rates, (b) Withholding Tax (q.v.), (c) Tax Amnesty (q.v.) and (d) stricter penal provisions.

An authorised tax officer can issue summons when he has reasons to suspect that any income has been concealed by any person within his jurisdiction. Summons is issued to enforce attendance of any person for the purpose of examining him. The person concerned may be examined to verify the authenticity of various types of transactions, the following being the common ones.

Capital Contributions: Summons can be issued to owners of a business (i.e. proprietors, partners and shareholders) to verify their capital contributions and sources of money thereof. Borrowed funds can be sources of money for capital contributions.

Business Transactions: An assessee makes claims in his return of income regarding purchases, sales, revenue expenditure and capital outlays. To verify such claims, the assessing officer can issue summons to suppliers, buyers and recipients of commissions, salaries, rent etc.

Borrowing of Funds: An assessee may borrow funds from institutional and/or non-institutional sources for various purposes. Borrowings from non-institutional sources (e.g. private moneylenders, relatives, friends etc.) may need to be confirmed by income tax authorities. Hence, summons can be issued to persons who have lent money to explain sources of money lent.

Investment Transactions: Summons can be issued to any person who has made substantial investments in shares, securities, land, buildings and costly consumer durables. The person so summoned is expected to explain with documentary evidence the sources of his funds. These sources may include borrowings, gifts received, property inherited, sale of jewellery etc. However, documentary evidence is necessary to prove these sources of money. It is advisable to reveal correct factual information which can be cross-verified. See also Tax Avoidance.

Tax Expenditures

These are provisions in tax laws pertaining to voluntary and involuntary activities of taxpayers. They are distinguished from Tax Incentives (q.v.) which deal only with the voluntary actions of the taxpayers. Thus, while all tax incentives are tax expenditures, all tax expenditures are not tax incentives. For example, under Section 88 of the Indian Income Tax Act, 1961, compulsory subscriptions to provident funds are eligible for Tax Credit (q.v.) in the same way as voluntary premiums paid for life insurance policies. The former, though tax expenditure, is not a tax incentive because it in no way influences the behaviour of an individual saver. The latter is a tax incentive as well as a tax expenditure.

Tax-free Shop **See Duty-free Shop**

Tax-free Zone

It is an area within the territory of a country in which customs duties and other indirect taxes are not applied. The area is used for export industries based on imported raw materials.

Tax-GDP Ratio

Level of taxation in a country is traditionally judged in terms of the ratio which taxes bear to some measure of national income. This ratio is called tax-GDP ratio and the change in it is determined by variations in both the numerator (total tax revenue) and the denominator (national income).

There are various problems associated with the definitions of numerator and denominator of tax-GDP ratio. For example, should profits/losses of public monopolies form part of the numerator? Should social security contributions be included in tax receipts? The denominator of the ratio suffers from more ambiguities because there are various measures of national income. Among the alternative measures of national income, the important ones are: Gross Domestic Product (GDP), Gross National Product (GNP), and Net National Product (NNP). Should taxes be related to GDP or GNP or NNP, and whether at market prices or at factor cost?

In choosing from the alternative measures of national income, the important considerations are: (a) the measure chosen should be readily available, (b) it is widely understood and (c) it is reliable. In view of these considerations, it is a common practice to use GDP at market prices as the denominator of the tax-GDP ratio. GDP is preferred because it avoids estimation of depreciation which is subject to various statistical and conceptual problems. For example, the Organisation for Economic Co-operation and Development uses GDP at market prices as the denominator for comparing tax-GDP ratios among its member countries.

Significance of Tax-GDP Ratio: The study of tax-GDP ratio is important because trends in taxation in a country or a group of countries are analysed mainly in terms of this ratio, and the composition of tax revenues. The latter may change owing to variations in tax-GDP ratio.

Tax-GDP ratio is generally regarded as an index of relative tax burden in a country over a period of time (time-series analysis) or when countries are compared for the same period (cross-section analysis). To describe tax burden in terms of tax-GDP ratio can be misleading because taxes, though burden for individuals, are used to finance vital governmental activities and to make transfers to needy sections of society.

What then does tax-GDP ratio signify? Since tax-GDP ratio indicates the percentage of national income that is compulsorily transferred from private pockets to public exchequer, and hence the relative share of government in the disposition of national income, it signifies the economic role of a government in the national economy. The ratio, however, does not reflect the importance of government sector as a final purchaser of goods and services because a part of tax revenue is returned to the private sector in the form of transfer payments like pensions and scholarships. If such transfer payments are deducted from the total tax revenue, the ratio of the remaining tax revenue to GDP will show importance of government as a final purchaser of goods and services. Since tax-GDP ratio reflects movements in both tax receipts and GDP, any significant revision in GDP figures will affect the ratio. Such revisions are not uncommon, particularly in developing countries, and therefore they indicate a limitation of the use of tax-GDP ratios. These cautions must be kept in mind while interpreting tax-GDP ratios.

Determinants of Tax-GDP Ratio: Tax-GDP ratio varies from country to country. What explains inter-country variations in tax ratios? The list of factors affecting tax ratio is almost inexhaustible. It includes a wide variety of economic, social, cultural and political factors. Broadly speaking, the variables explaining inter-country variations in tax ratio may be grouped under two categories: 1. Quantitative or statistical factors and 2. Qualitative or institutional factors.

Among the quantitative factors, the important ones are the following. These factors are crucial as they determine the tax bases which governments use to raise tax revenues. They are also the determinants of tax levels most widely used in empirical studies. They are believed to exert a strong influence over the tax ratio through their effect on what are called capacity factors.

1. Stage of Development: Stage of economic development is the first and foremost determinant of tax ratio. Economic development is a multi-faceted phenomenon affecting quality of life and therefore cannot be measured precisely by a single variable. Still, a variable frequently used as a proxy is per capita income which, though incomplete, is by far the single best indicator of the stage of economic development attained by a country.

It is usually hypothesised that per capita income and tax ratio move in the same direction, i.e. they are positively related. Presumably, people in countries with high per capita income require a smaller proportion of their income to meet their basic needs, and hence are left with a surplus which may be conveniently taxed. It is also argued that income elasticity of demand for public goods is high at high levels of per capita income. Moreover, since development process is normally accompanied by increasing urbanisation, high literacy rate, widespread monetisation, public consciousness and improved administration, the scope for taxation, particularly direct taxation, increases because all these factors are conducive to tax collection. However, in the context of inter-country comparisons, the use of per capita income as a determinant of tax ratio is subject to errors owing to the conversion of domestic currencies into US dollars. Moreover, the relationship between tax ratio and per capita income becomes decisive only after the latter has reached a minimum level, though it is difficult to define that level.

2. Composition of GDP: Another determinant of taxation level is the composition of GDP or the industrial origin of national output. Normally, a higher agricultural share in GDP is indicative of a lower per capita income, and hence a low stage of economic development. Thus, the proportion of income generated in the agricultural sector provides another index of the stage of development. Two countries may have the same level of per capita income but differences in the composition of their national output will affect their taxable capacities and tax ratios. Preponderance of agricultural sector means lack of industrialisation, existence of a large subsistence sector and administrative difficulties in implementing tax laws. Moreover, there is effective political resistance to taxation of agricultural sector. All these factors explain the negative influence of the agricultural sector on tax ratio.

Contrarily, the relative share of mining sector has a positive influence on tax ratio. As Roy Bahl has opined, "the mining sector generally produces a larger surplus than any other sector, and therefore it is a positive determinant of taxable capacity. Because of the heavy fixed investment associated with mining industries, operations will tend to be confined to a few large firms, and accordingly it will be administratively easier to levy income or export taxes."

Tax potential is greatly increased where industrial production dominates other sources of national income. Industrialisation is associated with urbanisation, banking transactions, accounting practices, all of which facilitate levy and collection of taxes. Some taxes (e.g. corporation tax) are directly linked with industrial activities.

3. Foreign Trade: Another determinant of tax level is the size of the foreign trade sector. It is presumed that taxable capacity increases with the expansion of external trade because it is administratively easier to tax trade inflows and outflows than internal transactions. Moreover, a relatively large size of external sector is indicative of greater degree of monetisation and organised industrial sector, both of which are favourable conditions for taxation.

There are three alternative measures of the size of foreign trade sector based on combinations of import and/or export share of GNP. These are: (a) import ratio (My), (b) export ratio (Xy) and (c) openness ratio, i.e. the ratio of imports plus exports (My + Xy) to GNP. Theoretically, the use of openness ratio is justified because it reflects the total trade base available for taxation.

4. *Composition of Government Expenditure:* If public expenditure pertains mainly to welfare activities (educational and medical services), it will favourably influence the general standard of living and hence the taxpaying capacity of the citizens. Conversely, if a large proportion of expenditure is devoted to defence and law and order, the taxpaying capacity will be reduced.

5. Pattern of Income Distribution: Two countries with the same level of per capita income may have different taxable capacities if the pattern of income distribution differs. Thus, size distribution of income becomes another determinant of tax ratio. It is widely believed that scope for taxation is greater when degree of concentration of income and wealth is higher. This is not always true because economic concentration implies more political power with the rich who effectively resist additional tax burdens upon themselves. For example, in India the near absence of agricultural income tax is mainly due to the preponderance of landlords and other vested interests in state legislatures.

Among the qualitative factors, the important ones are: efficiency of tax administration, attitude of the citizens towards government and its laws and ideology of the ruling party (e.g. left wing governments prefer a larger public sector). It is difficult to quantify the influence of socio-political factors on taxable capacity.

Recently, Vito Tanzi has called to attention the connection between tax levels and macroeconomic policies such as exchange rate, import substitution, trade liberalisation, inflation, public debt and financial policies. He believes that changes in tax levels cannot be attributed to traditional determinants alone, and greater attention should be devoted to the relationship between these macroeconomic variables and tax levels.

Factors influencing tax-GDP ratio are many and a variety of permutations and combinations can be used in empirical analysis. The choice of factors and their application is, however, constrained by the availability of data in a country.

Limitations of Inter-Country Tax Comparisons: Are inter-country comparisons of taxation levels meaningful? Some fiscal experts have sharply criticised these attempts. According to critics, the economic, political and institutional characteristics of individual countries are so different that neither theoretical nor empirical studies provide useful information of policy relevance. Tax-GDP ratios do not consider the fact that some countries are more favourably placed to levy and collect taxes than others. It is *prima facie* erroneous to compare Nepal's high rural and agricultural economy with a highly commercial and industrial city state of Singapore.

According to critics, the actual tax-to-income ratio is a vague concept because the definitions of numerator and denominator are debatable. In spite of these limitations, an outright rejection of international tax comparisons as meaningless is wrong. They are useful so far as they process and condense a large amount of otherwise incomprehensible information. However, it must be emphasised that such comparisons are more meaningful if attempted among countries having somewhat similar socio-economic circumstances.

Tax Haven

It refers to any country or locality which levies very low taxes, or none at all, on foreigners.

Tax havens can be broadly classified into three categories based on the degree of tax concessions. 1. Where there is no tax at all, e.g. Bahamas, Bermuda, and Cayman Islands. 2. Where only a low rate of tax is imposed, e.g. British Virgin Islands, Hong Kong, Isle of Man. 3. Where the tax system favours particular activities or entities, e.g. Luxembourg, Panama, and Switzerland.

Tax havens are used in a number of ways to avoid/evade high taxes of non-tax haven countries. The commonest device is to use a tax haven only as a conduit for transactions the real economic impact of which is located elsewhere. Thus, international transactions between two high tax rate countries may be channelled through a tax haven company so that any resulting profit is realised in the tax haven with a consequent minimisation of tax. See also International Tax Avoidance and Evasion; and Transfer Pricing.

Tax Holiday

It is a tax incentive targeted at new firms, and is not available to existing units. Under a tax holiday scheme, new enterprises are allowed a period of time free from the burden of income tax, subject to certain conditions.

Under Section 10A of the Indian Income Tax Act, 1961, a complete tax exemption is provided in respect of the profits and gains of an industrial undertaking set up in any free trade zone, electronic hardware technology park, or software technology park as specified by the Central Government for tax holiday. Complete tax exemption can be claimed in respect of any 5 consecutive assessment years falling within a time frame of 8 years beginning from the year in which the industrial undertaking commences production.

This tax concession is available to all categories of taxpayers. The tax holiday is in lieu of all other tax concessions available in the Act. Assessees availing tax holiday scheme are not entitled to other benefits such as set off and carry forward of losses, and deductions under various Sections of the Act. However, the assessees have the option to choose either the complete tax holiday scheme or all other tax concessions available under the Act.

Similarly, under Section 10B, any profits and gains made by an assessee from a 100 per cent export-oriented undertaking are not included in his total income. This benefit is available to an assessee in respect of any 5 consecutive assessment years (referred to as holiday period) falling within a period of 8 years beginning with the initial assessment year in which the undertaking commences production. Assessees availing this tax holiday scheme are not entitled to other tax concessions available in the Act.

Tax Impunity **See Tax Amnesty**

Tax Incentives

These are provisions in tax laws which encourage individuals and corporations to undertake activities desired by the government.

Almost all tax systems incorporate provisions which exclude certain items and deduct others from the tax base.

These provisions may take the form of exemptions, deductions, allowances, and tax credits. Tax incentives (or tax preferences) reduce the amount of tax which would otherwise be payable by a taxable entity. These tax preferences are referred to as tax incentives. Broadly speaking, items which erode the normally accepted base of a tax may be treated as tax incentives.

The form in which a tax incentive is given has implications of its own. Let us consider a tax concession given as a deduction from gross income rather than a credit against tax liability. The value of a deduction from gross income is less at low income levels and more at high income levels if a progressive rate schedule is applied. However, if the concession is granted as a credit against tax, the benefit will be equal for all taxpayers.

Rationale for Tax Incentives: Tax incentives, an integral part of tax systems the world over, are designed to promote a wide spectrum of socio-economic objectives. If judiciously used, they can become an effective tool of economic change on desired lines.

1. Individuals: Tax incentives related to individuals promote equity. Examples in this category are exemption of an initial slice of income from tax, and allowances related to dependants. Two individuals with equal incomes may have to support families of different sizes and it would be justifiable to extract less from the individual with a larger tamily size. However, these considerations are more relevant at low income levels. Apart from equity, promotion of individual savings, contributions towards charitable purposes are other commonly promoted objectives. Tax incentives for these purposes are usually in the form of deductions from taxable base or tax credits against savings/investments in specified channels.

2. Business Organisations: Tax incentives related to business sector are meant to induce business enterprises to undertake activities which they would otherwise shirk. Thus, these incentives are designed to encourage investment in general or in preferred industries or in preferred geographical areas (industrially backward regions). Such incentives take a variety of forms such as investment allowance, accelerated depreciation of fixed assets, and exemption of profits from tax for specified initial years of business (tax holiday).

3. General Purpose Incentives: These are meant to provide flexibility to the tax system to deal with changing market situations. They are used as a corrective mechanism to stabilise demand, production, and profits of different industries. Thus, tax incentives may be given to boost sluggish demand for idle-capacity industries. Similarly, incentives are given for the promotion of sports, cultural and social welfare organisations. Tax incentives are also given to promote exports, scientific research, and desired type of technology (e.g. labour-intensive technology in labour surplus economies). Thus, a tax system, apart from raising revenue, may be used to promote activities deemed vital by society, though it is controversial as to which activities are vital and require governmental support.

Problems Created by Tax Incentives: Tax incentives are often criticised for distorting economic activity. Incentives cause post-tax pattern of returns to diverge from pre-tax pattern and therefore lead to an allocation of resources different from the efficient equilibrium which the market is supposed to generate.

Tax incentives erode the taxable base and thus shrink government revenues. They introduce complexity into the tax system. Incentives require definitions of the eligible activities which in itself complicates tax legislation. By complicating tax laws, incentives increase the possibilities of tax evasion and litigation which in turn may adversely affect tax collections.

In case of individual assessees, tax incentives distort the incidence of a tax among different taxpaying classes and hence obscure its evaluation from equity angle. In fact, tax incentives distort the pattern of tax burden suggested by statutory rates. More specifically, tax incentives reduce effective tax rates below the statutory ones. Thus, statutory or nominal rates can be misleading when the redistributive effect of progressive rates is considered.

Tax incentives to a particular industry, which are often the result of persistent representation and pressure tactics, may lead to a chain reaction, i.e. similar demands by other industries, causing unsettling effects on producers, consumers, and the administration.

Alternatives to Tax Incentives: Tax incentives involve sacrifice of tax revenue and hence need to be devised carefully. The revenue foregone is similar to a subsidy or a grant to a taxable entity and hence akin to government expenditure. For example, there is no fundamental difference between an outright subsidy payment to a new industrial undertaking set up in a backward area and foregoing tax revenue on account of tax concession to it. However, outright subsidy payments attract public attention more readily than tax concessions (hidden subsidies) which lie scattered in the cobwebs of frequently changing tax laws. Thus, activities which deserve budgetary support should preferably be encouraged through expenditure programmes rather than the nebulous medium of tax incentives. The alternatives to tax incentives are: direct subsidies, government loans at subsidised interest rates, and foreign exchange facilities.

However, when support through tax concessions becomes necessary, their economic effects should be properly evaluated, i.e. whether the cost in terms of revenue foregone is justified by the likely benefits. In other words, a tax incentive should be appraised in the same way as any other item of public expenditure. The loss of revenue must be estimated on net basis because some increase in revenue may be attributable to stepped up economic activities due to tax favour. To what extent the intended positive effects (increased savings, investments, production etc.) of tax concessions are realised and to what degree they offset the negative effects (loss of revenue, equity distortions), are complex questions requiring rigorous empirical analysis.

Tax Incidence **See Incidence of Taxation**

Tax-inclusive and Tax-exclusive Basis for Taxation

The former is a rate of tax calculated on a tax base inclusive of the tax itself. It is contrasted with a rate of tax calculated on a tax base exclusive of the tax itself. A tax on personal incomes, and company profits is normally calculated on the tax-inclusive basis while an expenditure tax is calculated on tax-exclusive basis. For example, if tax authorities take away Rs. 400 from an income of Rs. 1000 leaving behind Rs. 600 for spending, it represents an income tax rate of 40 per cent calculated on a tax-inclusive basis. The corresponding (higher) rate of expenditure tax calculated on a tax-exclusive basis would be 66.6 per cent because a tax at this rate must be levied on Rs. 600 worth of expenditure in order to raise Rs. 400 in expenditure tax.

Tax Lien

It refers to a government claim on property for which taxes have not been paid when due. In extreme cases, the property may revert to the government.

Tax Loophole

It refers to an inadvertent oversight in the drafting of tax legislation. Such unintentional and unforeseen lapses and discrepancies in tax laws provide opportunities to clever taxpayers to avoid or reduce their tax liability. Sometimes, tax loopholes may be intentional to give special advantage to a particular activity or a class.

Tax Neutrality

It refers to a system of taxation that has no influence on the allocation of resources in the economy.

Tax Policy

Taxation is a potent instrument to shape and influence the socio-economic policies of a country. It is, of course, difficult to formulate a set of universally acceptable goals of tax policy because (a) different countries are in different stages of economic development, (b) objectives of economic policy differ in these countries, (c) priorities of economic policy are different, and (d) objectives and priorities of economic policy continually change with the changing economic, social and political milieu.

Though the concept of an ideal tax system for a country is linked with the peculiar characteristics of its economy, tax policy is usually assigned the following four functions in the stated order in a typical developing economy: resource mobilisation, resource allocation, distributive justice and stabilisation.

1. ***Resource Mobilisation:*** The first and foremost objective of tax policy in a country is to raise resources for public authorities for administration and development. Taxes are the main instrument for transferring resources from private to public use. By designing an appropriate tax structure, resources can be raised from those who are holding them idly or squandering them on luxury consumption. According to Roy Gobin, "the revenue criterion is usually the dominant consideration, since governments in LDCs have become increasingly aware of the active role which budgetary measures can play not only in initiating and promoting growth but also in maintaining political power. Not only are higher revenue levels needed, but also tax yields should be increased at a faster rate than income, if infrastructural investments and social welfare expenditures are to be financed without generating unacceptable inflationary pressures and/or increasing reliance on foreign assistance."

The revenue performance, i.e. resource mobilisation function of a tax system may be judged in terms of the responsiveness of tax yield to changes in macroeconomic aggregates like national income. Two widely-accepted measures of revenue performance are Buoyancy and Elasticity of Tax Revenue (q.v.).

2. ***Resource Allocation:*** Scarcity of real resources in developing countries calls for their optimum utilisation.

Since the composition of investment is an important determinant of growth rate of the economy, public policy must discourage the flow of resources to *low priority* areas so that they could be diverted to *vital* sectors of the economy. By imposing high tax rates on luxuries and other low priority items (such as motor cars, air conditioners and jewellery), the government can discourage the consumption and production of such items, ensuring in the process release of resources for high priority sectors. Conversely, production of necessities of life and employment-oriented industries can be encouraged by offering tax concessions or even subsidies.

3. ***Distributive Justice:*** Distributive justice or economic justice is an important function of tax policy. Economic justice relates largely to distribution of tax burden and benefits of public expenditure. It is a component of the broader concept of social justice which encompasses, besides distributive justice, such questions as treatment of women and children, and racial and religious tolerance in a society. Tax policy is a democratic method to influence the distribution of income and wealth on desired lines. The main ingredients of this policy can be (a) progressive direct taxation of income, wealth, and property transactions, (b) taxation of commodities (customs duty, excise levy and sales tax) purchased largely by high-income groups and (c) subsidies (negative taxation) on goods purchased by low-income groups.

Highlighting the importance of taxation and public expenditure policies in the context of redistribution of economic power, Alejandro Foxley has opined, "modern public finance studies have de-emphasised the analysis of the normative considerations of theory and focused on the very basic question of incidence: who pays and who benefits from government action? ... Thus we can say that focus has shifted from question of *what should the State do*? to the question of knowing *what in fact it has been doing*?"

4. ***Stabilisation:*** Initial developmental efforts are generally marked by inflationary tendencies in an economy. Inflation, if uncontrolled, may thwart all development plans and bring misery to the poor. A reasonable degree of price stability should be a primary concern of a government's economic policies.

The overall level of economic activity in an economy depends upon aggregate demand, relative to capacity output. At times, the level of aggregate demand may be insufficient to secure full employment of labour and other factors of production. At other times, aggregate demand may exceed available output at full employment level. Government intervention in both the cases becomes essential to correct such disequilibria in the economy.

Monetary and fiscal policies are important instruments available to the government to ensure smooth functioning of the economy. Reduction in taxes during deflation would leave greater disposable incomes with the people, giving a boost to aggregate demand. The reverse is true in times of inflation.

The evaluation of a tax system with reference to the foregoing objectives is a difficult task because various other policies (like public expenditure policy) may be geared to achieve the same objectives. To what extent the redistributive objective has been served and what was the relative role of tax policy in it, is a difficult question to answer. Moreover, the various objectives of tax policy may not always work harmoniously. Rather, they are often in conflict with each other if not mutually exclusive. Since the tax system of a country grows out of the interaction between political judgement and economic rationale, the process of compromises and trade offs is influenced by political expediency and economic logic, the former, in most cases, having the upper hand. In fact, political requirements and economic thinking change with time, giving new directions to tax policy. As Richard Bird has observed, "Tax reform is, therefore, a never-ending process, not something that can be brought about once and for all and then forgotten."

Tax Potential **See Taxable Capacity**

Tax Rebate **See Tax Credit**

Tax Rental Arrangement

A federal system of government creates a dual polity based on divided governmental functions and taxation powers. Tax laws of central government extend to whole of the country while those of the state governments are applicable within their respective jurisdictions. A tax belonging to the states may be imposed with varying base and/or rate in different states. Lack of uniformity in the imposition of state tax laws can cause difficulties for traders and consumers and thus hinder inter-state trade. To overcome these problems, arrangements could be made to transfer from the states, the legal right to levy the tax, to the centre with the proviso that revenue collected will be assigned to the states. This is known as a tax rental arrangement.

A tax rental arrangement has the following advantages. 1. It helps in maintaining uniformity in the prices of widely consumed goods throughout the country. 2. Such an arrangement contributes to the development of an integrated market by facilitating movement of goods across state borders. 3. Rationalisation of commodity taxation at the national level becomes easy. 4. Cost of collection is reduced.

Tax Secrecy

It refers to obligation on the part of tax officials not to disclose particulars about the identity, personal circumstances, and tax liability of taxpayers.

Tax Sharing

An arrangement whereby one level of government levies a tax and shares the proceeds with a lower level government.

There are two types of tax sharing mechanism. Under the first method (called global sharing), the entire tax revenue of the higher level government forms a pool for sharing with lower level governments. A certain percentage of the total tax revenue of the higher level government is allocated to lower level governments. The second method (called schedular sharing) involves sharing of revenue from individual taxes of higher level government. Tax sharing may take the form of a fixed amount or a fixed proportion of tax revenue. Formula-based tax sharing is a predictable source of revenue for the lower level governments.

Tax Shelter

It refers to devices whereby a taxpayer may invest earnings without paying income tax on them. Thus, subscriptions to provident funds, payments made towards life insurance policies, and pension plans are not considered income until they are paid out after maturity. It is almost synonymous with Tax Avoidance (q.v.).

Tax Shifting See Shifting of Tax

Tax Sparing Credit

Developing countries often give tax incentives, e.g. Tax Holiday (q.v.) to encourage foreign investments. Many developed countries provide in their double tax treaties with developing countries for a tax sparing credit. Under tax sparing, the investor is deemed to have paid the tax foregone in the country of source (say India) so that the investor's country of residence (say USA) grants a tax credit for the tax not charged by the source country. In other words, the residence country treats the income remitted as if it had been fully taxed and had not benefited from the tax incentives (of the host country). This ensures that the full benefit of the tax incentive goes to the investor and is not simply transferred to the residence country's treasury.

Tax Treatment of Family Income

A rather controversial issue in designing income tax system pertains to the treatment of income of spouses. If a husband and wife each earn a taxable income of Rs. 80,000 and Rs. 60,000 respectively, should the tax be assessed on the income of each of them separately or on the pooled income, i.e. Rs. 1,40,000? Under a progressive rate schedule, the combined tax liability of the couple will be less if their incomes are separately assessed rather than jointly taxed. A proportional tax system would make no difference whether the two spouses are taxed separately or jointly.

Separate taxation of the earnings of each spouse encourages marriages, causing a negative demographic effect in overpopulated countries. It also suffers from an individualistic view of life, a philosophy contrary to the social and cultural ethos of many societies. On the other hand, joint taxation puts unreasonable burden on two-earner families. Many governments have refrained from joint taxation of income fearing a backlash from women at the time of elections.

As a compromise, two procedures are generally followed to tax the income of a couple: (a) Splitting Method (q.v.) and (b) Quotient Method (q.v.).

Tax Treaty Shopping

The expression is used to describe a situation where a person resident in a third country seeks to obtain benefits of a Double Tax Treaty (q.v.) between two other countries.

A double tax treaty confers substantial benefits on the residents of treaty countries. Let us suppose that Mr. Wilson, resident in country A, wants to invest in country B. Assuming that there is no double tax treaty between country A and country B, any income received by Mr. Wilson will be subject to full rates of taxation in country B. In such a situation, Mr. Wilson may find it advantageous to channel his investment to country B through a company in country C because country C has double tax treaties with countries A and B. For example, Mauritius is a popular treaty shopping haven for many foreign companies for channelling investments into India because of favourable tax treaty provisions.

To prevent the misuse of tax treaties through tax treaty shopping, many countries take care to include anti-treaty abuse provisions in these agreements. For example, there is a specific clause in the double tax treaty between India and USA under which benefits of the treaty are available only to genuine residents of either country. In other words, the treaty restricts the use of USA as a treaty shopping centre for investments in India.

Tax Withholding See Withholding Tax

Tax Yield

It is the amount of money collected from a tax or a tax system. If the cost of collecting a tax is deducted from the gross tax yield, the resultant amount is net tax yield.

Tax yield is determined by (a) coverage of the tax, (b) exemptions/concessions, (c) rate structure, (d) tax compliance, (e) penal provisions and (f) administrative efficiency. There can be other factors also, specific to particular taxes. For example, the yield from excise duties also depends upon industrial progress and the general health of the economy. Similarly, revenue from customs duties is affected by factors like import policy, availability of foreign exchange and international trade climate.

Technological Dualism

Technological dualism refers to the use of different production functions in *modern* and *traditional* sectors of an economy. It is widely believed that labour employment problems of less developed countries (LDCs) are due to this dualism rather than due to lack of aggregate demand.

Traditional sector consists of peasant agriculture, handicrafts and cottage industries. Production can take place with a wide range of techniques, i.e. with various alternative combinations of labour and capital. Farmers can use simple tools and implements or heavy machinery for agricultural operations. Choice between capital-intensive and labour-intensive technology is available. Thus, this sector has *variable technical coefficients of production.*

Since labour is relatively abundant factor in LDCs, the technique of production is usually labour-intensive. The modern sector comprises large-scale industries, oil fields and mines. The technique of production is almost fixed. For example, if a modern oil refinery is to be set up, the proportion in which labour and capital are to be used is almost given (fixed). In other words, there is limited degree of technical substitutability. The technique of production in this sector is usually capital-intensive.

Technological dualism has been instrumental in aggravating disguised unemployment in the traditional sector. As surplus labour cannot be absorbed by the modern sector, it has to fall back on the traditional sector for survival. See also Economic Dualism.

Terms of Trade

They refer to the rate at which a country's exports exchange with its imports. It is, thus, the ratio of export prices to import prices. They are expressed as follows:

$$t = \frac{Xp}{Mp}$$

where t = terms of trade, Xp = export price index and Mp = import price index

Terms of trade depend on reciprocal elasticity of demand of the two trading countries for each other's commodities. If India's demand for German machinery is relatively less elastic than German demand for Indian textiles, then India's terms of trade will be unfavourable in the sense that given demand conditions, machinery prices will rise more than those of textiles. For the given amount of machinery, India will have to export more quantity of textiles.

Net Barter Terms of Trade: They are also called commodity terms of trade and expressed as follows: n = Xp / Mp x 100 where n = net barter terms of trade. For example, if there is an increase in India's export prices, there will be an improvement in commodity terms as India can obtain a larger volume of imports for the same amount of exports or India will have to export less for a given amount of imports. It indicates an improvement in a country's welfare.

Gross Barter Terms of Trade: Symbolically,

$$g = \frac{Mq}{Xq} \times 100$$

where g = gross barter terms of trade, Mq = import quantity index, Xq = export quantity index. An increase in import quantity index tends to improve gross barter terms while an increase in the export quantity index would tend to worsen these terms of trade.

Income Terms of Trade: If we consider both the prices of exports and imports and also the quantity index of exports we can know the value of exports, i.e. income derived from them. Thus, income terms of trade have the barter terms of trade and the export quantity indices, both put in one. Symbolically, i = n.Xq where i stands for income terms of trade. In other words,

$$i = \frac{\text{index of export value}}{\text{index of import prices}}$$

A rise in i means that the country concerned can get larger import volume than before from the sale of exports, i.e. country's capacity to import (based on exports) has increased. That is why it is also called *capacity to import index.*

Factoral Terms of Trade: Each commodity contains services of factors. Thus, there is a factor content in it. If we have to give more exports for a given volume of imports, it means more resources have to be given. This is a deterioration in trade conditions. To measure the correct situation, factoral terms of trade (S) are used. They are derived by multiplying net barter terms of trade index (n) by an index of productivity change in export industry (Xz)

If export industry becomes more efficient, less factors are needed in production. Hence S improves. This is, in fact, single factoral terms of trade. It is because only export industry's productivity is considered. But if we take into account productivity of import industry abroad also then we get double factoral terms of trade (D). Symbolically, D = Xz / Mz where Mz is the import industry's productivity. This index helps in knowing a comparative position of productivities in export and import industries. If productivity in export industry improves faster or more than in import industry, terms of trade are said to improve and vice versa.

Real Cost Terms of Trade: This concept takes into account the real cost of producing exports, i.e. the amount of utility lost per unit of resources sacrificed/employed in producing exports. Symbolically, $r = n.Xg / X_c$ where r = real cost terms of trade; Xg = export productivity index; and X_c = real cost of production of export goods.

If n falls but there is a corresponding increase in Xg, r will remain stable provided Xc is also stable. The situation will worsen if Xc also rises.

The problem here is the measurability of real cost which is difficult to know in clear quantitative terms. So the practical utility of r is very limited.

Territoriality Rule of Foreign Income **See Double Taxation**

Thin Market

The term refers to a relatively inactive market with a low-volume, low-value turnover.

Third World

In the context of international economy, this term is used for developing countries of Asia and Africa. Economists have grouped world economies into three main blocks, viz. (a) developed economies (first world) led by USA, UK, Japan, Germany and France, (b) former communist countries of East Europe (now in transition) led by the erstwhile USSR (second world) and (c) low-income developing countries (third world).

Tight Money **See Dear Money**

Time Wages **See Wages**

Tokyo Round

It refers to multilateral trade negotiations under GATT during 1973-79 which recommended tariff reductions, preferential treatment for developing countries, customs valuation code and a common approach to anti-dumping. Steps were taken to control the use of non-tariff barriers. Principle of non-reciprocity for developing countries was also accepted.

Toll

A toll (or octroi) is collected on goods that move into or through a local territory.

Total Cost **See Cost of Production**

Trade Creation and Diversion

Jacob Viner (1892-1970) introduced these concepts to analyse the effects of changes in trade patterns following creation of a Customs Union (q.v.).

Trade Diversion: After the formation of a customs union, free trade ensues among the member countries (say A and B) while imports from non-members (say country C) are subject to tariff. As imports from country C become costly due to tariff, country A shifts its imports from country C to country B. Suppose country C (the least cost world producer) is producing an item at Rs. 4 per unit while country B is producing it at Rs. 5 per unit. Also suppose Rs. 2 is the tariff rate per unit. Clearly, imports from country C now cost Rs. 6 per unit as compared to Rs. 5 per unit from country B. Thus, country A will divert its imports from country C to country B. This shift from least cost or most efficient producer in the world to the most efficient within the customs union is known as trade diversion. Obviously, there is a welfare loss to country A in this diversion.

Trade Creation: It results when, after the formation of a customs union, country A stops domestic production of high cost items and imports them from member countries who produce them more efficiently at relatively low cost. Hence, trade is created. As a result, there is a welfare gain to country A.

Trade Cycles **See Business Cycles**

Transfer Earning **See Rent**

Transfer Payments

Transfer payments are payments for which no goods or services are received in return. In other words, there is no *quid pro quo* in the case of transfer payments. Such payments include pensions, educational grants, unemployment allowances and gifts. These are unilateral payments the receipt of which by the concerned units is called transfer income. Some transfer payments are voluntary such as households giving donations to religious and charitable institutions. All taxes are forced transfer payments. Interest on public debt paid by the government is also a transfer payment.

Transfer Pricing

It is that price at which a parent firm (MNC) sells its product/technology to its subsidiaries in other countries. Alternatively, it refers to the price attached to transactions between the divisions (e.g. branches or subsidiaries) of a company. Transfer pricing is usually considered in a global context, particularly in relation to cross-frontier transactions within a multinational company.

Determination of transfer price has significance in relation to such matters as taxation, exchange restrictions, and currency fluctuations. The incentive for transfer price manipulations is provided by varying rates of taxation in countries where a multinational company operates. Thus, where goods are being transferred from a company in a low tax country to a subsidiary company in a high tax country, there is a clear tax incentive if a high transfer price is ensured to maximise profit within the low tax country.

Similarly, sales of a multinational group may be routed through a specially formed tax haven distribution company. The tax haven company purchases goods from affiliated companies at the lowest possible prices and sells to independent purchasers at the full market price, ensuring that most or all of the profit from the transaction is earned in the tax haven.

Due to the inherent difficulties in determining a fair or market price for inter-company transactions, a multinational company has always the option to fix artificial transfer prices. See also International Tax Avoidance and Evasion; and Tax Haven.

Transfer Tax See Stamp Duty

Transformation Curve See Production Possibility Curve

Transnational Corporation (TNC) See Multinational Corporation

Treaty of Montevideo

After various negotiations among Latin American countries held at Montevideo, Mexico City and Bogota during 1961 to 1964, a treaty was signed at Montevideo which opened the doors for the establishment of Latin American Free Trade Area (LAFTA).

Tripartite Trade Agreement

It is an agreement on trade matters to achieve certain ends concluded among three countries.

Turnover Tax

It is a tax on transaction of goods and services at all levels of production and distribution. It is levied every time that a commodity, whether semi-finished or finished, changes hands. The result of a general turnover tax is to pyramid the amount of the tax from one stage to another so that the final selling price of the commodity includes the sum of all taxes paid during the production and distribution of the commodity. When a turnover tax is in operation, it is to the advantage of producers and distributors to avoid as many independent transactions as possible.

Two-tier Exchange Rate See Exchange Rate

U

Unbalanced Growth

It is a strategy of economic development advocating deliberate unbalancing of capital investment in favour of strategic industries. A chronic imbalance of investment, it is argued, will generate incentives and pressures in non-strategic industries, leading to faster rate of growth of the economy as a whole in the long-run. See also Balanced Growth.

Uncertainty-bearing Theory of Profit See Profit

Underemployment

This is a situation under which people work less than they would like to work. These people may be working on daily, weekly or monthly basis.

Underwriting See Stock Market

Undistributed Profits Tax

It is imposed on companies which allow their retained profits to accumulate beyond the reasonable needs of business. Companies may prefer to hold profits rather than pay dividends so that their shareholders could postpone personal income taxes that would have to be paid if the dividends were paid out. Undistributed profits tax attempts to checkmate this practice on the part of companies.

Unearned Income See Earned and Unearned Income

Unemployment

Unemployment is a situation when willing workers fail to get jobs at the prevailing wage rates. From social point of view, unemployment means wastage of the precious labour resources of the country. For an individual, unemployment is a painful and demoralising experience.

Urban unemployment : Urban unemployment may be classified into two categories: (a) industrial unemployment and (b) educated unemployment. Industrial unemployment is the result of slow growth of industrial development vis-à-vis growth of labour force. Tendency on the part of rural people to migrate to cities in search of employment further leads to competition in the job market. Another facet of urban unemployment is the lack of job opportunities for the educated people. University degree holders and even professionally trained people find it difficult to get jobs.

Rural Unemployment : Unemployment in the agricultural sector is the most serious aspect of unemployment problem in developing countries. First of all, there is open unemployment among the landless agricultural workers. There is also considerable disguised unemployment in the agricultural sector. Farming is a family occupation. Small-sized farms employ more workers than needed. Even if some hands are withdrawn from the farm, total output is not affected. According to American economist Ragnar Nurkse (1907-1959)), disguised unemployment exists when marginal productivity of labour, over a wide range, is zero. Yet another dimension of rural unemployment is the problem of seasonal unemployment. Agriculture by its very nature provides seasonal employment. For a significant part of the year the farmer is out of work. In the absence of supplementary sources of employment, he has to remain unemployed during the slack season.

Structural Unemployment: As economic growth proceeds in an economy, there are changes in the pattern of demand. Some industries suffer a decline in demand (e.g. jute industry in India) while others enjoy an increase in demand (e.g. synthetic fibre industry). Such permanent shifts in demand patterns require economic readjustment in the absence of which structural unemployment occurs.

Causes of unemployment are various and include labour force pressure, slow growth of the economy, capital-intensive technology and defective education system. The solution of the problem of unemployment lies in reversing the causes of unemployment. It means controlling the population growth, speeding up the pace of industrialisation, adoption of labour-intensive technology and making the education system job-oriented.

Unequal Exchange, Theory of

It states that there is a transfer of reinvestible surplus from the low wage labour-abundant developing countries to the high wage capital rich industrial countries through unfavourable and unequal terms of trade for the former. It adds to the poverty of the less developed countries.

Units of Assessment

It means persons or taxable entities chargeable to tax under a tax law. For example, under the Indian Income Tax Act, 1961, there are seven units of assessment: 1. An individual, 2. A Hindu Undivided Family (HUF), 3. A company, 4. A Firm, 5. An association of persons or a body of individuals whether incorporated or not, 6. A local authority and 7. Every artificial juridical person, not falling within any of the preceding categories.

Unit Tax **See Specific Duty**

United Nations Commission on International Trade Laws (UNCITRAL)

It is a commercial code drafted by UNCITRAL for use in all international transactions.

United Nations Conference on Trade and Development (UNCTAD)

It is a semi-autonomous body of United Nations with headquarters in Geneva. Considering that GATT was dominated by USA and West European countries, developing countries (Group of 77) felt the need for a separate platform to discuss their problems. In 1964, these countries initiated UNCTAD during meetings for several weeks in Geneva.

In 1968, another Conference was held in New Delhi with focus on trade problems and prospects of development. It was known as UNCTAD-II. Since then, UNCTAD has been discussing and bring out various schemes like indexation, common fund for price stabilisation of primary products etc.

United States Agency for International Development (USAID)

It was established in 1961 by President John F. Kennedy. It provides assistance for economic development and humanitarian purposes to advance economic and political interests of USA overseas.

Unsecured Loan

It is a loan which is not secured on any property/assets. Contrarily, a secured loan/debt is guaranteed by assets.

Unstable Equilibrium **See Stable and Unstable Equilibrium**

User Charge

It is a fee or charge for use of a government-supplied service, generally transportation service. It is applied so that those who benefit from public transport services repay the cost to the government. User charges are usually in the form of tolls, licence fees and fuel taxes and fall on highway and waterway traffic.

Ushr

It is a tax imposed on agricultural produce under Islamic law for charitable purposes. In Pakistan, *Ushr* was imposed in 1983 at the rate of 5 per cent.

Utility

Utility is the satisfying power of a commodity. A commodity is demanded because it can satisfy a particular want of the buyer. Bread has utility because it can satisfy hunger. Utility is an abstract phenomenon and hence non-measurable.

Utility is a psychological phenomenon concerned with the state of mind of the consumer. Being subjective, utility of a commodity is not the same for all individuals. A commodity may have more utility for one person, less for another, and no utility for yet another.

Utility of a commodity varies with its quantity. As one consumes more of a commodity, the successive units give less and less utility. This is called the *law of diminishing marginal utility.* The significance of this law is that it helps to explain the equilibrium of the consumer. Since the income of a consumer is limited, he has to make choices and these choices must be made in such a way that total satisfaction is maximised.

According to the *law of equi-marginal utility*, a consumer should spend his income so that the marginal utility derived from the last unit of money spent on various commodities is the same.

V

Value Added Tax (VAT)

Value added tax is levied on the sellers of goods and services based on value added by their respective units. The base of VAT is determined by value added at a particular stage of production or distribution. Meaning of VAT becomes clearer when it is juxtaposed against conventional turnover tax (excise duty, sales tax) which falls on the total value of the product at each stage of production chain and is called a *cascade* type tax.

VAT, a fiscal innovation of early 1960s, has claimed world-wide attention as more and more countries are adopting it in varying degrees to reform their system of commodity taxation.

Origin of VAT: Pursuant to the Treaty of Rome (March 25, 1957), the European Economic Community (EEC) was set up with the primary objective 'to establish, within the framework of an economic union, a common market providing for healthy competition and having characteristics similar to those of an internal market.'

From July 1, 1968, all customs duties and quotas in trade between EEC member countries were abolished to move towards a common market with equality of competition as a condition. Following the principle of destination, exports to member countries became entirely tax free, and imports from countries within the community began to be treated in the same way as domestic production destined for home consumption.

To follow the above policy, two arrangements had to be made. 1. Although tax on export of goods as such was abolished, the possibility of taxation of these goods during various stages of their production and distribution still existed. The rules of the new arrangement demanded calculation and refund of tax burden on goods as and when they were classified as exports. 2. Imports into the country, which had escaped taxation by claiming refund in the exporting country, needed to be taxed in a way which avoided discrimination between them and domestically produced goods which had already faced taxation at different stages. Therefore, it was necessary to replace with a common system the differing systems of indirect taxes which had distorted competitive conditions between the member states.

With the above purpose in view, the Commission of the EEC had set up a Committee under the chairmanship of Professor Fritz Neumark which submitted its findings entitled *Report of the Fiscal and Financial Committee of EEC* in 1962. The Neumark Report visualised ultimate acceptance by all EEC countries of all-stage value added tax similar in terms of tax rates, exemptions etc.

Agreeing with the recommendations of the Neumark Report, the Council of Ministers of the six original EEC countries issued two directives dated April 11, 1967 which required the common market states to abolish the existing gross turnover tax systems and to introduce a comprehensive system of value added taxation by January 1, 1970. Value added tax, an offshoot of economic union, therefore emerged as an instrument of tax harmonisation in the EEC countries. It was a fiscal necessity in the absence of which the success of common market experiment would have been seriously hampered. In certain cases its adoption was almost a precondition for entry in the common market (e.g. UK replaced purchase tax and selective employment tax by VAT with effect from April 1, 1973). Though VAT grew as an offshoot of economic union of EEC countries, it has been adopted voluntarily in many countries as a measure to rationalise commodity taxation.

Value Added and VAT: Value added at a particular stage is measured through two alternative approaches: (a) subtraction method and (b) additive method. Both these approaches are based on the identity that total sale proceeds of a firm from its output during a given period are equal to the cost of inputs, wages, rent, interest, depreciation and profits.

Under the subtraction method, value added is measured by deducting value of inputs from the value of output (O-I). If the cost of inputs is deducted from total proceeds, the remainder represents the sum of factor incomes plus depreciation.

Alternatively, additive method adds together various types of factor incomes generated, and depreciation. In practice, subtraction method is considered more handy and therefore widely relied upon.

There are two ways to compute VAT according to subtraction method. Under the first method, called the *sales less purchases* or *accounts* procedure, the rate of tax is multiplied by the difference of output and inputs, t (O-I). Under the second method, called the *tax credit* or *invoice* procedure, the product of the rate of tax and input is deducted from the product of the rate of tax and output, t (O) - t (I). The latter is more common in practice being the system applied throughout EEC countries. The VAT liability of a seller under it is equal to the tax arising from its total sales minus a credit for the tax paid by it on its purchases. The seller charges full tax from his buyer but pays to the government the difference between the tax charged and the one already paid on his (seller's) inputs.

Treatment of Depreciation Under VAT: There are three ways to treat the cost of capital goods whose use in the production process is spread over time.

1. Since value added is defined as output minus input, it is necessary to clarify whether input includes depreciation of capital goods. One interpretation is that it does, i.e. depreciation (also called capital consumption) is excluded from the value added so that value added reflects the sum of wages, interest, rent and profits. This is called the *income variant approach* under which the base for taxation is net value added by each producer. The net value added is defined as gross receipts minus purchases of intermediate goods and depreciation. This corresponds to the concept of net national product in national accounting.

2. The second approach is to exclude the cost of capital goods from value added instead of granting allowance for depreciation over the life of capital goods, and is called the *consumption variant approach*. Value added is now defined as gross receipts minus purchase of intermediate products and capital expenditure on machinery etc. Since producers are allowed to deduct their capital expenditures, the base for taxation is restricted to the value of production of consumer goods only.

3. Lastly, it is possible that the cost of capital goods is not allowed to be excluded when they are initially purchased and no allowance is made for depreciation when they are used in production. Value added equals gross receipts minus

the cost of purchasing intermediate goods. In other words, it is the sum of wages, rent, interest, profits and depreciation. This may be called the *gross product variant* and is the most comprehensive form of VAT. It corresponds to the gross national product concept of social accounting.

The consumption variant approach permits a firm to deduct purchases of capital goods (i.e. gross investment) while income variant concept allows it to deduct depreciation only. In this sense, the base for VAT is bigger under the income variant than under the consumption variant by the amount of net investment (gross investment minus depreciation).

In brief,

Income variant = Gross receipts - Cost of intermediate goods - Depreciation

Consumption variant = Gross receipts - Cost of intermediate goods - Cost of capital goods

Gross product variant = Gross receipts - Cost of intermediate goods

Benefits and Limitations of VAT: VAT is a multi-stage tax levied on all stages of production and distribution of a commodity. It is collected in instalments on the basis of value added at each stage of production and distribution of a commodity. It is a comprehensive levy covering almost all production and distribution in its fold. It is different from excise duties which, in many cases, are selective in nature.

Under VAT, each input is taxed only once. Since an input is taxed only once, VAT avoids *cascading* which is the chief disadvantage of the traditional system of excise and sales taxation. Excise duties and multi-point sales taxes levied on gross output tax the same input repeatedly as goods pass along different stages of production. This type of taxation encourages vertical integration of industries, a tendency harmful to the growth of small-scale sector.

Since the cumulative effect of input taxation is absent under VAT, the cost of production increases by the amount of tax itself. Thus, by preventing unnecessary cost escalation, VAT promotes competitiveness of domestic industries in the world market and thereby generates favourable effects on exports.

VAT in its ideal and comprehensive form also has the advantage of being neutral as between different industries, techniques of production, and business organisations. Therefore, it does not distort patterns of production and consumption. However, neutrality of a tax is not always desirable particularly in the context of an underdeveloped country which has to use its scarce resources in the best possible manner.

Among the various limitations of VAT, the following are more common: VAT is levied on *ad valorem* basis and does not admit of physical output as the basis for tax liability determination. Excise duties may be imposed on *ad valorem* or specific or *ad valorem*-cum-specific basis, or even in the form of a compounded levy.

Ideally, VAT should be imposed at a uniform rate at all stages of production and distribution so that tax credit claims can be made easily. Excise duties, as also sales taxes, are imposed at different rates depending upon the nature of the commodity taxed.

VAT is more suitable under a unitary form of government, i.e. under a single tax authority for commodity taxation. In a federation where different tiers of government enjoy overlapping commodity taxation powers, VAT is difficult to operate due to tax rivalry and lack of co-ordination among federal and provincial governments.

VAT and Evasion: The proponents of VAT claim that evasion under it is difficult and minimal. The tax credit method ensures cross-checking of the records of taxpayers through invoices. Buyer firms insist on supplier firms to furnish invoices which help the former to claim tax credit. Since tax liability of a single taxpayer under VAT is only a fraction of the total amount of tax, the incentive for evasion is relatively weak. Even a successful evasion would mean less revenue loss as compared to the one suffered under a system of turnover (excise or sales) tax on gross value.

In spite of the self-policing nature of VAT, opportunities do exist under it for evasion and fraud. In fact, VAT provides opportunities for fraud (fictitious claims for refunds) which are not available under other forms of commodity taxation. The methods commonly applied to defraud tax authorities under VAT include, *inter alia,* the following.

1. Use of fake invoices to claim tax credit.
2. Tax credit claims on purchases for personal use.
3. Over-reporting of sales of zero-rated goods.
4. Secret deals between buyers and sellers as regards issuance of receipts.
5. Formation of fake companies which sell receipts to traders to enable them to claim tax credit on inputs.

In short, VAT is as susceptible to evasion and fraud as any other tax. An efficient tax machinery capable of cross-checking a large number of invoices through an elaborate computer system is a pre-requisite for the successful implementation of VAT. This is precisely what is lacking in an underdeveloped country.

Administration of VAT: A comprehensive VAT requires an elaborate system of book-keeping, involving numerous computations, at each level of production and, therefore, may prove very cumbersome for the taxpayers. It calls for additional and efficient administrative efforts to check and cross-check the paperwork done by the taxpayers. VAT requires both a collection and a refund mechanism. Apparently, both collection and compliance costs have a tendency to increase. The problem of administration is more serious in developing countries where accounting practices are less developed, partly due to low literacy rate. It is much simpler for firms to file returns of gross turnover than the value added returns which require, *inter alia*, accounts of taxes paid on inputs. This problem is further compounded because of the preponderance of small-scale producers and sellers in less developed economies. These constraints deprive VAT of its theoretical advantage of automatic cross-checking to discourage evasion. Lack of proper recording of transactions and the unmanageable number of small taxpayers engage the administration in a futile exercise of hide and seek. This problem can partly be solved by extending the VAT system to wholesale stage only and exempting sectors dominated by small-scale production. For further simplification, VAT may be restricted to the manufacturing stage. Exclusion of retail and wholesale stages would significantly reduce burden on administration without, at the same time, interfering in the working of the tax since they come at the end of the production chain.

Value of Output

Each producing enterprise purchases raw materials and hires factor inputs to produce commodities. Evaluation of commodities produced by it at the prices prevailing in the market is called *value of output (or gross output) at market prices.*

Goods used for intermediate consumption were not produced but purchased by the enterprise from some other enterprises. If the value of intermediate consumption is deducted from the value of output at market prices, we get gross value added at market prices.

Gross value added at market prices = Value of gross output at market prices - value of intermediate consumption

From the gross value added at market prices, if consumption of fixed capital is deducted, we arrive at net value added at market prices. Thus,

Net value added at market prices = Gross value added at market prices - consumption of fixed capital.

Again, from the net value added at market prices, if net indirect taxes are deducted, we get *net value added at factor cost.* It is the cost to the producing enterprise for the net value added and income to the factor owners. Thus, net value added at factor cost is equal to the factor incomes: rent, wages, interest and profits, By adding up the net values added of all the enterprises, we get net value added in the domestic territory.

Variable

A variable is a symbol (say x) which can assume any of the prescribed set of values, called the domain of the variable. If that symbol can assume only one value it is called a constant. If a phenomenon can only be counted but not measured, it is an attribute. Thus, an attribute is the presence or absence of a given characteristic. An outcome of an event such as the birth of a child leads to an observation of an attribute of sex, i.e. *male, not male*. In this case, attribute is equated with the concept of a *qualitative* or *binary* or *dummy variable*.

Discrete and Continuous Variables: A variable which can theoretically assume any value between two given values is called a continuous variable. In general, continuous variable involves measurement as, for example, the height of a person.

A variable which can take only discrete or exact values is called a discrete variable. In general, discrete data involve enumeration or counting, e.g. cricket score, family members etc.

Exogenous and Endogenous Variables: An exogenous variable (also called autonomous variable) is one that influences other variables within a theory but is itself determined by factors outside the theory. Conversely, an endogenous variable (also called induced variable) is one that is explained within a theory.

Random and Non-random Variables: Variables whose values cannot be fully controlled or determined prior to observation (e.g. outcome of tossing a coin) are called *random or stochastic variables*. In contrast, a non-random or non-stochastic or fixed variable is one that is fully controllable or at least fully predictable. A constant may be regarded as a special case of a fixed variable.

Variable Cost **See Cost of Production**

Variable Proportions, Law of **See Diminishing Returns, Law of**

Variable Technical Coefficients of Production See Technological Dualism

Vehicle Currency

It refers to that currency which acts as a medium of exchange in the foreign exchange market as, for example, US dollar. Exchange rate between two currencies is often determined through it.

Veil of Money

According to this concept, money is merely a medium of exchange and hence neutral. Behind the money transactions lies the real process, i.e. exchange of goods for goods. People often fail to see through the veil of money and consider money as having value in itself. See also Money Illusion.

Velocity of Circulation See Equation of Exchange

Vent for Surplus Theory of Trade

According to this theory propounded by Adam Smith (1723-1790), a country exports its surplus goods. Trade provides a *vent* to this surplus or excess productive capacity that would otherwise remain unused. As domestic resources were not being fully employed before trade, trade raises the level of domestic production and thereby the level of national income.

Venture Capital

It is a term used for investment made in those lines where risk elements is very high, especially in new lines of production, new markets or new processes.

Vertical Compensation **See Loss Carry Forward**

Vertical Equity

It is a tax equity criterion advocating that unequals be taxed unequally. See also Ability-to-Pay Principle of Taxation.

Vertical Fiscal Imbalance

Although a federal system provides for divided governmental functions and powers, imbalances often (rather invariably) arise between functional responsibilities and financial resources at different levels of the government. This is so because revenue-raising capacities and revenue needs of various federating units are different. This is a characteristic feature of all federations, particularly those whose economies are more dynamic. Even in older federations (like USA, and Canada), financial conflicts persist between the national, state, and local governments and their once-for-all solution is unachievable.

The mismatch between functions and financial powers occurs partly because of changing responsibilities of different tiers of the government and partly due to the dominant position of the national government with regard to taxation powers, which is often by design. Therefore, vertical imbalances of resources and expenditure responsibilities emerge between different levels of government, calling for transfer of resources from the centre to the states, and from states to local bodies. This is a familiar problem of federal finance.

Vertical financial imbalances are sought to be removed/reduced through constitutional arrangements, and in some countries through political bargaining as well.

Vertical Foreign Investment

It occurs when a parent multinational corporation decides to establish foreign subsidiaries to produce intermediate goods or inputs that go into the production of finished goods. It contrasts with the production of identical good in the host country in which case it is horizontal investment.

Visible Trade

It is the merchandise trade (exports and imports of physical commodities) as distinct from invisible trade (services like banking, insurance and transport).

Volumetric Duty See Specific Duty

Vostro Account

A foreign bank's account with a local bank is called vostro account. For example, pound sterling account of a French bank with a London bank is a vostro account as far as London bank is concerned.

W

Wages

Wages are payments made for the services of labour of any kind. Labour being an active factor is the most crucial of all factors of production. Adam Smith (1723-1790), leader of the classical economists termed labour as the source of all wealth.

Labour population of a country is classified into the following groups: (a) Skilled Workers: These include doctors, engineers, aircraft pilots and other highly trained persons. They receive education and training for a very long period of time. (b) Semi-skilled Workers: In this category are placed workers who are moderately educated and trained to perform their jobs. Thus, truck drivers, typists and nurses are semi-skilled workers. (c) Unskilled Workers: This category includes workers of the ordinary type as, for example, sweepers, porters and watchmen.

The term wages has a variety of connotations.

Money and Real Wages: Money or nominal wages refer to the amount of wages measured in terms of money. In economics, the term money wages is used to represent the labour cost of production of a commodity. Real wages refer to the amount of goods and services which a worker can buy with his money wages.

Piece Wages and Time Wages: Piece wages are paid on the basis of quantity of work done. A tailor may be paid a certain amount for each shirt stitched in a particular fashion. Piece wages are possible only where the work is uniform and the worker's output is easily measurable. Time wages are paid on the basis of length of time as, for example, monthly wages. Time wages do not bear close relationship between earnings and output as is the case with piece wages. Employers generally favour piece wages while employees prefer time wages.

Wages in kind consist of payments to the worker, not in the form of money, but in the form of commodities.

Wage Rate Determination: How wages get determined in the market? There are various explanations to this question right from the days of classical economists.

Subsistence Theory of Wages: This theory was propounded by economists in the early 19th century. At that time population was rapidly increasing in Europe but food supplies were relatively short. This phenomenon led the economists to believe that the supply of labour, over the long-run, was perfectly elastic (horizontal supply curve of labour). Thus, every increase in wage rate would be pulled down to the original level by increase in population and labour supply. This original level was conceived as the minimum amount, i.e. the amount which was just sufficient to maintain the worker and his family. They called it the subsistence level of wages. In the long-run wages always equalled the cost of subsistence. Any rise in wages would result in proportionate increase in population. This theory is also called the *iron law of wages*.

Wage Determination under Perfect Competition: Wages under perfect competition are determined in terms of demand for and the supply of labour. The demand for labour originates from industrial firms. As in the case of any other commodity, the higher the price (wage) of labour the lower the demand for it and vice versa. Contrarily, the higher the wage rate the larger the amount of labour supplied and vice versa. By the interaction of the forces of demand and supply, wage rate for the industry is determined. For each firm in the industry, this wage rate is given.

Reasons for Differences in Wages: Wages are the reward for the services of labour. However, wages of all types of workers are not the same. Differentials in wage rate are due to a host of factors.

1. Wages differ with the type of job. Generally, more risky jobs carry more wages than less risky jobs involving same skills. Coalminers get more wages than ordinary ditch-diggers.

2. Wages depend on the length of education and training required to perform a particular job. A surgeon gets more than a typist because the job of the former requires education and training for a much longer period than the job of the latter.

3. Wages vary with experience in a particular job. An airline pilot with 20 years experience gets more than a newly recruited pilot.

4. Wage differentials may exit due to sexual and racial prejudices. Very often women get less wages than men for doing the same job. Similarly, black workers may be paid less than the white workers.

5. Wages also differ according to the structure of the labour market. In a competitive market, wages are less than in an imperfect labour market. Members of strong trade unions earn more than their less organised counterparts. See also Backward-bending Supply Curve of Labour.

Wagner's Law of Increasing State Activity

In 1883, a German economist Adolph Wagner (1835-1917) propounded his famous *law of ever increasing state activity*. He based his conclusions on an extensive survey of public expenditure records of several countries in the 19th century. Although he did not make it clear as to what he precisely meant by increasing state activity, it is generally believed that he was referring to growth in public expenditure as a percentage of national income.

Wagner put forward three reasons for the operation of his law. 1. He believed that an expansion would come about with respect to the administrative and protective functions of the state. This would require substitution of public for private activity. As a result of industrialisation there would be greater division of labour, communications and legal complexities. All this would increase the regulatory and protective activities of the government. 2. The pressure for social progress was thought to be another reason for the expansion of state activities. He anticipated considerable expansion of cultural and welfare expenditure, particularly with respect to education and the redistribution of income. 3. Changes in technology and the large amount of investment required in many economic activities would create private monopolies. The state would be required to offset the effects of these monopolies in the interest of economic efficiency. In certain cases as, for example, railways, only state could finance the scale of investment required.

Wagner's law of expanding state expenditure has received extensive comments from economists the world over. Various empirical studies have given conflicting evidence regarding the validity of Wagner's law. Frederic Pryer in his study of government expenditures has concluded that neither highly developed nor highly underdeveloped countries fit Wagner's generalisations. According to Pryor the law appears to be supported for countries in the process of transition from a rural agricultural economy to an urban industrial one.

American public finance expert Richard Musgrave, on the other hand, has supported Wagner's law in his study of public expenditures of Germany, USA and UK.

Though the evidence on Wagner's formulation remains puzzling, one drawback of his analysis is definite, viz. his neglect of war expenditure. It has specially been noted by economists that Wagner took no particular note of the effects of wars on public expenditure. Probably in tune with the 19th century optimism he anticipated fewer wars in the future than in the past. However, he was proved grossly wrong by the events of the subsequent years. Unfortunately, major international conflicts have dominated lives and patterns of public expenditure in the 20th century. Any theory of public expenditure which ignores wars and their effects must be termed incomplete in its scope. Thus, while Wagner's law may appear to hold good in aggregate terms, serious doubts arise regarding its validity if studied in disaggregated form. See also Peacock-Wiseman Hypothesis.

Warranty

This is an increasingly important tool in international business these days. It attests the supplier's commitment to quality and after-sale services (maintenance facilities, spare parts etc.).

Ways and Means Advances

These are short-term loans (also called floating debt) made by the central bank of a country to the government of that country. The purpose of ways and means advances is to accommodate temporary mismatch in the receipts and payments of the government.

Wealth Tax

Wealth represents the command a person has over economic resources at any point of time. Tax base for purposes of wealth tax is normally the taxpayer's net wealth i.e. total assets less liabilities. The base is generally modified by exemptions and deductions.

The tax may be imposed on companies or individuals or both. Similarly, the tax may be imposed at either a flat rate or at a progressive rate.

Wealth tax is advocated on both benefit and ability-to-pay considerations. Protection of life and property has traditionally been a primary function of the government and to perform the same, considerable cost is incurred on law enforcement machinery and judicial administration. The main beneficiaries of these services are the people with fabulous wealth who, as a rule, should contribute towards the expenses on such services. Pavement sleepers hardly need the services of the state as protector of property. Another dimension of the benefit argument is that public services like roads, street lighting, community centres, public parks etc., increase the value of real estates, conferring unearned benefits on the owners of such estates. Therefore, it can be argued that property owners should pay for these services.

In terms of ability-to-pay, possession of property is a measure of economic well-being and therefore of taxable capacity, quite apart from the income earned from that property. A tax on capital itself may seem undesirable when capital income is subject to income tax (as is generally the case). However, the coverage of capital income under income tax is usually incomplete in view of liberal exemptions, tax avoidance and evasion. Moreover, an income tax system does not include non-earning assets. Therefore, taxation of wealth is essentially a supplement to taxation of income. Hence, taxation of wealth is justified on equity criterion. It may be argued that wealth tax is unjust in cases where property does not yield money income directly. In this context British tax expert Nicholas Kaldor (1908-1986) opined, "If a property does not yield money income, it must either yield an equivalent psychic income to the owner or it must be held in the expectation of a certain appreciation in value which makes it at least as attractive to the holder as other property on which a current money return is obtained."

Yet another argument for taxation of wealth is social control over the most unjust and dangerous form of economic inequality. To quote Richard Musgrave, "Alternatively, the taxation of wealth may be approached not as a matter of charging for benefits received or ability-to-pay, but as a form of social control. The social consequences of inequality in the distribution of wealth, as is easily seen, differ from those in the distributions of consumption, so that society may wish to deal with them separately. For this purpose, a progressive tax on wealth, rather than on income, is the proper instrument." Situations may arise when certain taxpayers have taxable wealth but very low current income. One way to resolve this problem is to exempt from wealth tax liability all those taxpayers whose annual income from all sources does not exceed a specified limit.

In spite of being a potentially important source of revenue and economic control, the administration of wealth tax is difficult, particularly in the case of developing countries.

Imposition of wealth tax requires the preparation of an annual balance sheet of assets and liabilities of the taxpayer. For an honest exercise of this sort, an assessee should first declare, truthfully, all taxable assets with their proper current value. He must also make a genuine claim for deductible debts. Honesty of the sort required is an exception rather than the rule. Thus, tax officials for most of their part are busy detecting taxable assets, grappling with undervaluation of properties and verifying claims of deductible debts. Some of these problems (e.g. valuation of assets) are encountered also in connection with estate duty, capital gains tax and local property tax. Valuation of assets for purposes of one tax is generally used as a basis for computing tax liability under another tax. However, the continuous rise in prices (leading to appreciation of real estates), underdeveloped nature of money markets (causing difficulty in the valuation of shares), and the ingenuity of tax evaders, leave the tax authorities groping in the dark without much success.

Welfare Economics

Welfare economics deals with the evolution of alternative economic situations from the standpoint of society's well-being. Let us denote the present total welfare in a country as W. We suppose that with given resources and technology, W can be increased to W*. The task of welfare economics is two-fold: (a) to establish that in the present state $W<W^*$ and (b) to suggest ways and means to increase W to W* .

On what basis do we evaluate alternative economic situations from welfare angle? Various criteria of social welfare have been suggested by economists from time to time. Some important ones among these are described below:

GNP Growth as Welfare Criterion: Since economic growth implies increased availability of goods, it may be accepted as a criterion of social welfare. In other words, increase in GNP means bringing W closer to W*.

There are, however, various limitations with this criterion. Firstly, it assumes a given distribution of income which may or may not be equitable. Secondly, it does not reveal the beneficiaries of the growth process. It is likely that in the growth process the distribution of income worsens and total social welfare is reduced. In spite of these limitations, the growth criterion retains some utility as it highlights the importance of efficiency in raising GNP and hence social welfare. However, efficiency, though a necessary condition, is not a sufficient condition for maximisation of social welfare.

Bentham's Criterion: According to Jeremy Bentham (1748-1832), social welfare is improved when the greatest good is secured for the greatest number. Obviously, this rule implies that the total welfare of society is the sum of the utilities of the individuals. Such a reasoning has serious limitations in practical application. To explain these limitations, we assume that the society consists of three individuals, A, B and C so that

$$W = U_A + U_B + U_C$$

According to Bentham

$$\triangle W > 0 \text{ if } (\triangle U_A + \triangle U_B + \triangle U_C) > 0.$$

It is possible that A's and B's utility increases while C's utility decreases so that $(\triangle U_A + \triangle U_B) > \triangle U_C$. In other words, A and B are better off while C is worse off after the changes. Or, the sum of the increases in utilities of A and B is greater than the decrease in the utility of C. Is the changed situation better for the society as a whole, i.e. all the three individuals considered together? It is difficult to draw any definite conclusion since it involves interpersonal comparison of welfare of the three individuals.

Cardinalist Criterion: The use of the law of diminishing marginal utility is also proposed as a criterion of social welfare. Suppose a society consists of three individuals such that A has an income of Rs. 1,000 while B and C have an income of Rs. 500 each. Individual A can buy double the quantities of goods as compared to B and C. However, given the law of diminishing marginal utility, A's total utility is less than double the total utility of either B or C. To increase social welfare, income should be redistributed among the three individuals. In fact, social welfare would be maximised if income is equally distributed among all members of the society.

The shortcoming of the cardinalist approach is apparent. It assumes that all individuals have identical utility functions for money. This assumption is too restrictive because individuals differ in their attitudes toward money. Furthermore, the welfare effects of an equal distribution of income cannot be examined in isolation from the effects on resource allocation and the incentive for work of individuals. An equal income distribution may induce some people to work less.

Kaldor-Hicks Compensation Criterion: Kaldor-Hicks approach to welfare criterion may be understood with the following example. Suppose a change in the economy is being considered which will benefit some (gainers) and hurt others (losers). One can ask the gainers how much money they would be prepared to pay in order to have the change. Similarly, we may ask the losers how much money they would be prepared to pay in order to prevent the change. If the amount of the money of the gainers is greater than the amount of the losers, the change constitutes an improvement in social welfare, because the gainers could compensate the losers and still have some net gain.

Kaldor-Hicks criterion evaluates alternative situations on the basis of monetary valuations of different persons. Thus, it implicitly assumes that the marginal utility of money is the same for all the individuals in the society. Given that the income distribution is unequal in the real world, this assumption is absurd. In fact, this criterion makes implicit interpersonal comparisons since it assumes that the same amounts of money have the same utility for individuals with different incomes. This is not plausible.

Bergson Social Welfare Function: Bergson has suggested the use of a social welfare function similar to the individual consumer's utility function. It provides a ranking of alternative situations in which different individuals enjoy different utility levels. If the economy consists of two individuals the social welfare function can be presented by a set of social indifference curves, as shown in the Figure below.

In the Figure below, each curve is the locus of combinations of utilities of A and B which yield the same level of social welfare. The higher a social indifference curve is, the higher the level of social welfare will be. With such a set of social indifference curves, we can evaluate alternative situations in the economy. For example, a change which moves the economy from point b to point c (or d) increases the social welfare. A change moving the society from a to b leaves the level of social welfare unchanged.

The problem with the social welfare function is that there is no easy method of constructing it. Somebody in the economy must undertake the task of comparing the various individuals or groups and rank them according to their worthiness. This is an impossible task.

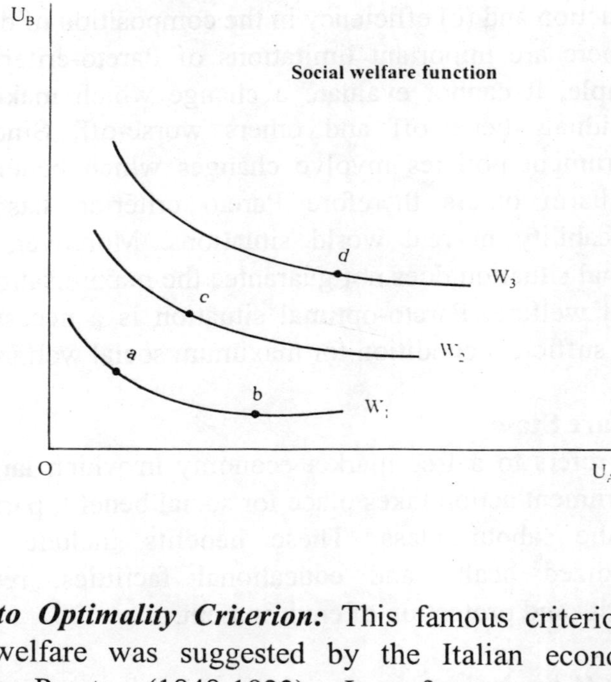

Pareto Optimality Criterion: This famous criterion of social welfare was suggested by the Italian economist Vilfredo Pareto (1848-1923). It refers to economic efficiency which can be objectively measured. The Pareto optimality (or Pareto efficiency) criterion may be defined in the following different ways.

Any change which makes at least one individual better-off and no one worse-off is an improvement in social welfare. Conversely, any change which makes no one better-off and at least one worse-off is a decrease in social welfare. To put it differently, a situation in which it is impossible to make anyone better-off without making someone worse-off is said to be Pareto-optimal or Pareto-efficient.

There are three marginal conditions which must be satisfied for the attainment of Pareto-efficient situation. These are: (a) efficiency in exchange, (b) efficiency of production and (c) efficiency in the composition of output.

There are important limitations of Pareto-criterion. For example, it cannot evaluate a change which makes some individuals better-off and others worse-off. Since most government policies involve changes which benefit some and harm others therefore Pareto criterion has limited applicability in real world situations. Moreover, Pareto-optimal situation does not guarantee the maximisation of the social welfare. Pareto-optimal situation is a necessary but not a sufficient condition for maximum social welfare.

Welfare State

It refers to a free market economy in which large-scale government action takes place for social benefit, particularly for the labour class. These benefits include free or subsidized health and educational facilities, retirement benefits and protection of environment.

***What If* Analysis**

International trade environment keeps on changing. Therefore, exporters and importers are always concerned with the nature, size and direction of such changes and how to face them. What if it really happens? How to cope with the new situation? What if analysis recognises the complexities, discontinuities and uncertainties of the real world and offers possibilities to traders to tackle them.

Withholding Tax

It is a system of collecting income tax whereby money is periodically deducted by the employers, financial institutions, and others from wages of employees, returns on securities, and other payments. Thus, intermediaries (or third parties) do the job on behalf of the government as regards assessment of the taxable base and the collection of tax thereon.

Generally, a fixed percentage is withheld from the payment made and the same is deposited in the government's account. At the time of filing the return of income, the taxpayer encloses withholding tax receipts, and in case of overpayment can claim refund of tax.

Tax withholding system (also called tax deduction at source or Pay-As-You-Earn) satisfies the canon of convenience both for the fiscal authorities and the taxpayers. It is beneficial for the government because it reduces the possibility of tax evasion, ensures prompt tax payment, and simplifies tax collection. It does not allow any lag between the time of receiving income and the time of tax payment. For the taxpayer, it is an instalment plan of taxation and hence convenient.

However, tax withholding involves additional paper work on the part of tax deductors. It also adds to the burden of taxpayers who have to obtain tax deduction certificates from deductors, fill additional tax forms, and wait for refunds. See also Advance Tax Payment.

Work Force Participation Rate

Total population of a country may be divided into two categories: (a) working population and (b) non-working population. The size of working population or work force is important in relation to the level of economic activities. This is so because labour being an active factor of production, is the source of all wealth.

The size of labour force is determined by the number of people in the age group 15-60 years. Traditionally, children below the age of 15 and old persons above the age of 60 are excluded from the definition of work force. The work force participation rate in a country depends on factors such as age composition, sex ratio, attitude toward work, and availability of employment opportunities. Apparently, these factors differ from country to country.

In 1991, 37.5 per cent of the total population was categorised as working population in India. In other words, the ratio between working to non-working population was 37.5:62.5. Work participation rate for male population was 51.5 per cent and for female female population 22.2 per cent.

World Bank **See International Bank for Reconstruction and Development**

World Customs Organisation **See Customs Cooperation Council Nomenclature**

World Trade Organization (WTO)

Basic Facts

Location	Geneva, Switzerland
Established	January 1, 1995
Created by	Uruguay Round negotiations (1986-94)
Membership	132 countries
Budget	$ 93 million
Secretariat staff	500

WTO is expected to

(a) administer WTO trade agreements,
(b) provide forum for trade negotiations,
(c) handle trade disputes,
(d) monitor national trade policies,
(e) provide technical assistance and training for developing countries and
(f) co-operate with other international organisations.

The eighth round of multilateral trade negotiations held under GATT and lasting for seven years (1986-1993) named Uruguay Round, resulted in new legal agreements for trade and strengthening settlement system. Following this, there was a Ministerial conference in Marrakesh, Morocco in April 1994 attended by 125 government representatives from across the world to sign for the establishment of a new successor institution of GATT, namely the World Trade Organization (WTO). It is an embodiment of the Uruguay Round results. WTO entered into force on January 1, 1995, with all assets and liabilities of GATT transferred to the former. Geneva was to be its headquarters.

All GATT committees were superseded by WTO committees. Initially, there are four sub-committees: (a) budget, finance and administration, (b) institutional, procedural and legal matters, (c) trade and environment and (d) services.

WTO ensured that each member country negotiates with its trading partners its terms of entry into the multilateral trading system and a market access schedule for goods and services. All the contracting parties (member countries) pledged to make every effort to quickly conclude domestic ratification of the WTO Agreement.

Broadly speaking, WTO has set to continue negotiations and bring agreements in the following areas:

1. Basic telecommunications.
2. Maritime transport.
3. Movement of natural persons.
4. Financial services.
5. General Agreement on Trade and Services (GATS).
6. A reaffirmation of the rule of law in trade and economic relations.
7. A reversal of long standing protectionist practices in agriculture, textiles and clothing.
8. An extension of multilateral rules to services and intellectual property rights.

WTO's creation in 1995 marked the biggest reform of international trade since 1948. During those 47 years, international commerce had come under GATT which helped establish a prosperous multilateral trading system. However, by the end of 1980s an overhaul was due.

The Uruguay Round brought about that overhaul. It was the largest trade negotiations ever. At times the talks seemed doomed to fail, but in the end the Uruguay Round was successful. The task was so immense that some people wondered whether there would ever be another negotiations like these. Was it the round to end all rounds?

WTO is GATT plus a lot more. GATT (the institution) was small and provisional, and not even recognised in law as international organisation. It has now been replaced by the WTO. GATT (the agreement) has been amended and incorporated into the new WTO Agreements. GATT dealt only with trade in goods. WTO Agreements cover services and intellectual property as well.

WTO is the only international body dealing with the rules of trade between nations. At its heart are the WTO agreements, the legal ground rules for international commerce and for trade policy. The agreements have three main objectives: (a) to help trade flow as freely as possible, (b) to achieve further liberalisation gradually through negotiations and (c) to set up an impartial means of settling disputes.

A number of simple, fundamental principles run throughout all the WTO agreements. They are the foundation of the multilateral trading system. They include: non-discrimination, freer trade, predictable policies, encouragement to competition and extra provisions for less developed countries.

The economic case for an open trading system based on multilaterally agreed rules is simple enough and rests largely on commercial common sense. However, it is also supported by evidence. Protectionism leads to bloated inefficient companies and can in the end lead to factory closures and job losses. One of the WTO's objectives is to reduce protectionism.

WTO is run by its member governments. All major decisions are made by the membership as a whole, either by ministers (who meet every two years) or by officials (who meet regularly in Geneva). Decisions are normally taken by consensus. The highest authority is the ministerial conference which meets at least once every two years. More routine work is supervised by the General Council. Numerous other councils, committees, working parties and negotiating groups cover the wide range of WTO issues.

Written Down Value

It is the value of a depreciable asset determined by deducting from the actual cost the depreciation allowances granted by income tax authorities in previous tax years.

Actual cost - Depreciation = Written down value

Following is a hypothetical numerical example to calculate written down value.

	(Rupees)
Cost of machine installed on September 15, 2000	80,000
Less: Depreciation of the previous year (2000-01) @ 30 per cent	24,000
Written down value on April 1, 2001	56,000
Less: Depreciation of the previous year (2001-02) at the same rate	16,800
Written down value on April 1, 2002	39,200

X

X-efficiency

The concept of X-efficiency, attributed to Harvey Leibenstein, is an important issue in economic development. It is basically concerned about why people do not work as hard or as effectively as they could. In other words, X-efficiency deals with how human inputs affect economic development. X-efficiency is generally contrasted with allocative (or static) efficiency.

Y

Yaounde Convention

This was a convention of European Common Market countries and those from former Afro-Asian colonies along with twenty other developing nations. The convention finalised Yaounde Agreement which came into force on January 1, 1964 and provided for mutual trade preferences with special trading arrangements for developing countries. However, this Agreement came in for criticism as it provided for reciprocity which the ex-colonies and the developing countries were not in a position to honour.

York-Antwerp Rules

They refer to an international set of regulations governing maritime shipping designed to help settle disputes arising from losses. They often are incorporated in shipping contracts.

Young Plan (1929)

Named after Owen D. Young, it fixed total German reparations at US $ 7.83 billion in contrast to Dawes Plan (q.v.) which did not set any particular figure. Germany was freed from foreign financial supervision. Bank for International Settlement (q.v.) was set up at Basel to receive the payments in German marks and manage their transfer to the beneficiaries.

Z

Zakat

It is a Koranic tax imposed annually on Muslims in Islamic countries, mostly in the Middle East. It is levied on the liquid assets of a person and is used for the benefit of the poor. In the wake of the movement towards an Islamic economy launched in Pakistan in 1979, *zakat* was deducted from all deposits and saving accounts in the banks at the rate of 2.5 per cent per annum beginning June 1980.

Zazia

It is an Islamic direct tax of the nature of a Poll Tax (q.v.). In India, under some Mohammedan kings, *zazia* or capitation tax was levied on all non-Muslims in lieu of military service which was required of all Mohammedans.

Zero-base Budgeting (ZBB)

Credit for this fiscal innovation goes to Peter Pyhrr who propounded it in the early 1970s in the context of corporate industrial organisations. The idea soon caught the fancy of Jimmy Carter, the then Governor of Georgia, who became the first to adopt ZBB approach to government budgeting in the 1973 budget of that State. When he became President he mandated the Federal bureaucracy to prepare USA budget for the year 1979 on the basis of ZBB. Since then a number of state governments in USA have followed suit by adopting ZBB in varying degrees depending upon their local requirements and conditions.

Under ZBB, each item of expenditure is challenged for its very existence in every budget cycle and no base or minimum expenditure level is presumed for any activity. Zero-base budgeting means the past is cut off, the present is regarded as a clean slate and all departments have to start from a scratch (hence zero-base). It is also called sunset budgeting, meaning that the sun would set on each governmental activity after a specified period. Before the sunset date, each department would be required to present ZBB, indicating achievements of its activities and what would result if the activities were not renewed.

Essential Elements of ZBB: There are three essential elements which distinguish ZBB from conventional budgeting.

Firstly, under the conventional system, departments (called budget units) may prepare and submit budgets which group many important activities under one head, making it difficult to scrutinise each activity closely. As against this aggregative approach, ZBB requires budget units which are small enough to allow close examination of their programmes. ZBB puts under magnifying glass the nature of activity of each budgetary unit. For example, in case of the health department, a separate budget needs to be prepared for controlling each disease instead of for the whole department. Once the budget unit's activity is identified, the ZBB procedure asks: what if the activity were not funded at all? And are there other ways to perform the activity and meet the unit's objectives? The onus of explanation lies squarely on departmental heads who are responsible for the activity and for preparing its budget.

Secondly, ZBB assumes that even if an activity needs to be financed it can be financed at a lower-than-current level.

In other words, economy in public expenditure on acceptable public activities is at the heart of ZBB's second essential rule. It requires evaluation and review of all programmes and activities, current as well as new, and believes that those who are incharge of public spending have the capacity to cut down expenditure without affecting the current level of public services.

Thirdly, ZBB requires priority-ranking among competing services of a budgetary unit. This ranking is done by listing all elements of a decision package in order of decreasing benefit to the community. High priority services are ranked at the top followed by low priority services until all are ranked. The list so prepared is used to fund services in order of priority until available resources are exhausted. Many of the services at the fag end of the list may just be eliminated for want of funds.

In brief, the three essential principles of ZBB are the following: (a) should we spend? (b) how much should we spend? and (c) where should we spend?

Limitations of ZBB: Application of ZBB has various limitations. Many activities of the government may be mandatory within the existing political framework and may even lie outside the jurisdiction of the legislature. For example, in India emoluments and allowances of the President, and Judges of the Supreme Court and High Court are beyond the vote of the Parliament. Furthermore, ZBB becomes unrealistic in case of many other public services which defy application of cost-benefit analysis owing to their very nature. Defence services, law and order, and maintenance of foreign relations are cases in point. It is clear that the application of ZBB has to be selective rather than governmentwide. ZBB is an approach not a fixed procedure to be applied uniformly from one type of expenditure to another or one level of government to another. The procedure must be adapted to suit the specific needs of each department.

The major threat to ZBB approach emanates from bureaucrats because it evaluates the effectiveness of their decisions and exposes their programmes to critical public review. This new idea in public budgeting requires effective administration, communication, and training of personnel involved in the analysis. It increases paperwork considerably and one frequent complaint against ZBB is that legislators seldom find time to scrutinize the analytical exercises done by the bureaucracy. In any event, ZBB is a long-term budgetary reform and its introduction has to be done in a phased manner. See also Budget.

Zero-bracket Income

It is that amount of taxable income which is taxed at a rate of zero per cent. The United States Federal individual income tax allows $3,400 of tax-free income to a married couple if it does not opt for Itemised Deductions (q.v.). This is accomplished by taxing the first $3,400 at a rate of zero, hence the zero-bracket rate. Those who do itemise, subtract from gross income only the excess of their itemised deductions over the zero-bracket amount.

Zero-rated Goods

Under Value Added Tax (q.v.), there are sometimes zero-rated goods like food, newspapers and medical prescriptions. For such goods, no VAT is charged on output but VAT suffered on inputs is reclaimable. Hence, zero-rated goods escape entirely from VAT. On the other hand, there are services like postage, education, and health which are exempt from VAT. No VAT is charged on these services but no VAT can be reclaimed on inputs. Hence, exempt goods do not suffer any tax on the value added at the final stage.

Zero-tax Company

Income tax laws usually provide for a host of deductions and incentives to promote socio-economic objectives of state policy. It is likely that a profit-making company may arrange its affairs in such a way that the cumulative effect of all deductions is to reduce its income declared in the tax return to zero. To deal with such situations, some countries have introduced Minimum Alternative Tax (q.v.).

Zoolverein

It is a popular German word for Customs Union (q.v.). It is also called Deutsche Zoolverein.

Appendix 1
Country Composition by Regional Grouping

Europe

EFTA (European Free Trade Association)
Iceland Switzerland Norway

EU (European Union)
Austria Belgium Denmark France Finland Germany Greece Ireland Italy Netherlands Luxembourg Portugal Spain Sweden United Kingdom

America

Andean Group
Bolivia Columbia Ecuador Peru Venezuela

CACM (Central American Common Market)
Costa Rica El Salvador Guatemala Honduras Nicaragua

CARICOM (Caribbean Community)
Antigua and Barbuda Bahamas Barbados Belize Dominica Grenada Guyana Jamaica Montserrat Saint Kitts and Nevis Saint Lucia Saint Vincent and the Grenadines Trinidad and Tobago

LAIA (Latin American Integration Association)
Argentina Bolivia Brazil Chile Colombia Ecuador Mexico Paraguay Peru Uruguay Venezuela

MERCOSUR (Southern Common Market)
Argentina Brazil Paraguay Uruguay

OECS (Organisation of Eastern Caribbean States)
Antigua and Barbuda Dominica Grenada Montserrat Saint Kitts and Nevis Saint Lucia Saint Vincent and the Grenadines

Africa

CEPGL (Economic Community of the Great Lakes Countries)
Burundi Rwanda Zaire

ECCAS (Economic Community of Central African States)
Burundi Cameroon Central African Republic Chad Congo Equatorial Guinea Gabon Rwanda Sao Tome and Principe Zaire

ECOWAS (Economic Community of West African States)
Benin Burkina Faso Cape Verde Cole d'Ivoire Gambia Ghana Guinea Guinea-Bissau Liberia Mali Mauritania Niger Nigeria Senegal Sierra Leons Togo

MRU (Mano River Union)
Guinea Liberia Sierra Leone

PTA (Preferential Trade Area for Eastern and Southern Africa)
Angola Burundi Comoros Djibouti Eritrea Ethiopia Kenya Lesotho Madagascar Malawi Mauritius Mozambique Namibia Rwanda Seychelles Somalia Sudan Swaziland Uganda United Republic of Tanzania Zambia Zimbabwe

UDEAC (Central African Customs and Economic Union)
Cameroon Central African Republic Chad Congo Equatorial Guinea Gabon

UEMOA (West African Economic and Monetary Union)
Benin Burkina Faso Cote d'Ivorie Mali Niger Senegal Togo

UMA (Arab Maghreb Union)
Algeria Libyan Arab Jamahiriya Mauritania Morocco Tunisia

SADC (Southern African Development Community)
Angola Botswana Lesotho Malawi Mozambique Namibia Swaziland South Africa United Republic of Tanzania Zambia Zimbabwe

Asia

ASEAN (Association of South East Asian Nations)
Brunei Darussalam Indonesia Laos Malaysia Myanmar Philippines Singapore Thailand Vietnam

Bangkok Agreement (First Agreement on Trade Negotiation Among Developing Member Countries of ESCAP)
Bangladesh India Lao, People's Democratic Republic of Korea Sri Lanka

ECO (Economic Co-operation Organisation)
Afghanistan Azerbaijan Iran, Islamic Republic of Kazakhistan Kirgyzstan Pakistan Tajikistan Turkmenistan Turkey Uzbekistan

GCC (Gulf Co-operation Council)
Bahrain Kuwait Oman Qatar Saudi Arabia United Arab Emirates

SAARC (South Asian Association for Regional Co-operation)
Bangladesh Bhutan India Maldives Nepal Pakistan Sri Lanka

Interregional

ACP (African, Caribbean and Pacific States signatories of the Lome Convention)
Angola Antigua and Barbuda Bahamas Barbados Belize Benin Botswana Burkina Faso Burundi Cameroon Cape Verde Central African Republic Chad Comoros Congo Cole d'Ivorie Djibouti Dominica Dominican Republic Equatorial Guinea Eritrea Ethiopia Fiji Gabon Gambia Ghana Grenada Guinea Guinea-Bissau Guyana Haiti Jamaica Kenya Kiribati Lesotho Liberia Madagascar Malawi Mali Mauritania Mauritius Mozambique Namibia Niger Nigeria Papua New Guinea Rwanda Saint Kitts and Nevis Saint Lucia Saint Vincent and the Grenadines Samoa Sao Tome and Principe Senegal Seychelles Sierra Leone Solomon Islands Somalia Sudan Surinam Swaziland Togo Tonga Trinidad and Tobago Tuvalu Uganda United Republic of Tanzania Vanuatu Zaire Zambia Zimbabwe

APEC (Asia Pacific Economic Co-operation)
Australia Brunei Darussalam Canada Chile China Hong Kong Indonesia Japan Korea, Republic of Malaysia Mexico New Zealand Papua New Guinea Philippines

Singapore Taiwan, Province of China Thailand United States of America

NAFTA (North American Free Trade Area)
Canada Mexico United States of America

Appendix 2

Country Composition by Economic Grouping

Nations are commonly classified into groups that indicate their economic strengths and weaknesses as well as their stage of development. Industrial or developed nations are those which have achieved substantial manufacturing and service capability in addition to advanced techniques in agriculture and raw material extraction. Developing nations are usually those whose production sector is dominated by agriculture and mineral resources and are in the process of building up industrial capacity. typically, these sectors not cnly serve home markets but also product for exports. The objective is to try to earn funds from selling abroad in order to have buying power available for future purchases of foreign goods and services.

Much attention in international economic and political affairs understandably focuses on the welfare gap between the developed and developing nations. Comparisons are frequently made among countries concerning such measures of economic progress and competitive strength as cultivated land area, population, per capita income and wealth, unit labour costs, prices, external debt, and monetary reserves. The emerging countries with resources and expanding industrial capability, e.g. Brazil, Korea, Mexico, and Taiwan, are more and more called the new industrial countries (NICs). The generalisation is often made that most of the richer nations are located in the Northern Hemisphere and the poorer nations in the Southern Hemisphere. This gives rise to the expression "North/South" in reference to many international problems, confrontations, and dialogues.

Most of the trade of the world occurs between the industrialised countries. The remaining nations strive to strengthen their economies by trade, barter, aid, and concessions from the major developed nations. The petroleum-rich countries, particularly the Organisation of Petroleum Exporting Countries (OPEC), control much of the world's immediately available energy resources which the industrial nations need in order to keep their economies functioning.

Major Petroleum Exporters

Algeria Angola Bahrain Brunei Darussalam Congo Ecuador Gabon Indonesia Iran, Islamic Republic of Iraq Kuwait Libyan Arab Jamahiriya Nigeria Oman Qatar Saudi Arabia Syrian Arab Republic Trinidad and Tobago United Arab Emirates Venezuela

Major Exporters of Manufactures

Brazil Hong Kong Malaysia Mexico Republic of Korea Singapore Taiwan Province of China Thailand Turkey Yugoslavia (former)

High Income Countries

(Year 2000 per capita GDP above 3,500 US dollars)

American Samoa Antigua and Barbuda Aruba Bahamas Bahrain Barbados Bermuda British Virgin Islands Brunei Darussalam Cayman Islands Cyprus French Polynesia Gabon Greenland Guadeloupe Guam Hong Kong Iran, islamic Republic of Iraq Korea, Republic of Kuwait Libyan Arab Jamahiriya Malta Martinique Montserrat Nauru Netherlands Antilles New Caledonia Omen Puerto Rico Qatar Reunion Saudi Arabia Seychelles Singapore

Taiwan Province of China Trinidad and Tobago United Arab Emirates Yugoslavia (former)

Middle Income Countries

(Year 2000 per capita GDP between 700 - 3,500 US dollars)
Algeria Angola Argentina Belize Bolivia Botswana Brazil Cape Verde Cameroon Chile Christmas Island Colombia Congo Cook Islands Costa Rica Cole d'Ivoire Cuba Djibouti Dominica Dominican Republic East Timor Equador Egypt El Salvador Falkland Islands (Malvinas) Fiji French Guyana Grenada Guatemala Honduras Indonesia Jamaica Jordan Lebanon Macau Malaysia Mauritius Mexico Morocco Namibia Niue Pacific Islands Panama Papua New Guinea Paraguay Peru Philippines Saint Helena Saint Kitts and Nevis Saint Lucia Saint Pierre and Miquelon Saint Vincent and the Grenadines Samoa Senegal Solomon Islands Surinam Swaziland Syrian Arab Republic Thailand Toketau Tonga Tunisia Turkey Turks and Caicos Islands

Appendix 3
National Currencies of 161 Countries of the World

The global monitoring system is now dominated by the United States Dollar. The British pound, the German mark, Japanese yen, the Swiss franc are also key currencies. A number of other money units play important roles in specific local markets. The physical transfer of actual paper money, coins, gold and silver bullion, and travellers' cheques among nations is small compared with the massive volume of credit, deposits, and investment funds moving daily across boundaries.

Each national currency necessarily has a value for international exchange purposes. A host of developments, including economic and political news and confidence, will influence the value of a currency. Through time, economic performance, reserves, and the relative rate of inflation seem to be among the most important determinants of value.

London, New York, Singapore, Tokyo, and many other global cities constitute important financial centres which, linked by close communications enable nations and the overall world economy to function around the clock to serve people.

Country	Currency
Afghanistan	Afghani
Albania	Lek
Algeria	Dinar
Argentina	Peso
Armenia	Dram
Aruba	Aruban Florin

Australia	Aus. Dollar
Austria	Schillings
Azerbaijan	Manat
Bahamas, The	Bahamian Dollar
Bahrain	Dinar
Bangladesh	Taka
Barbados	Barbados Dollar
Belarus	Rubel
Belgium	Franc
Belize	Belize Dollar
Benin	Franc
Bhutan	Ngultrum
Bolivia	Boliviano
Botswana	Pula
Brazil	Reai
Burkina Faso	Franc
Burundi	Franc
Cambodia	Riel
Cameroon	Franc
Canada	Canadian Dollar
Cape Verde	Escudo
Central African Republic	Franc
Chad	Franc
Chile	Peso
China P.R.	Yuan
China - Hong Kong	HK Dollar
Colombia	Peso
Comoros	Franc
Congo D.R.	New Zaire
Congo, Rep of	Franc
Costa Rica	Colone
Cote d'Ivoire	Franc

Croatia	Kuna
Cyprus	Pound
Czech Republic	Koruny
Denmark	Kroner
Djibouti	Franc
Dominica E. Carribbean	Dollar
Dominican Rep.	Peso
Ecuador	Sucre
Egypt	Pound
El Salvador	Colone
Equatorial Guinea	Bipkwele
Estonia	Krooni
Ethiopia	Birr
Fiji	Fiji Dollar
Finland	Markkaa
France	Franc
Gabon	Franc
Gambia, The	Dalasi
Guinea-Bissan	Franc
Germany	Deutsche Mark
Ghana	Cedi
Greece	Drachma
Grenada E. Carribbean	Dollar
Guatemala	Quetzale
Guinea	Franc
Guyana	Guyana Dollar
Haiti	Gourde
Honduras	Lempira
Hungary	Forint
Iceland	Kronur
India	Rupee
Indonesia	Rupiah

Iran I.R.	Rial
Iraq	Dinar
Ireland	Pound
Israel	New Sheqalim
Italy	Lira
Jamaica	Jamaica Dollar
Japan	Yen
Jordan	Dinar
Kazakhstan	Tenge
Kenya	Shilling
Korea	Won
Kuwait	Dinar
Lao PDR	Kip
Latvia	Lats
Lebanon	Pound
Lesotho	Loti
Liberia	Liberian Dollar
Libya	Dinar
Lithuania	Litai
Luxembourg	Franc
Madagascar	Franc
Malawi	Kwacha
Malaysia	Ringgit
Maldives	Rufiyaa
Mali	Franc
Malta	Lira
Mauritania	Ouguiya
Mauritius	Rupee
Mexico	New Peso
Moldova	Lei
Mongolia	Tugrik
Morocco	Dirham

Mozambique	Meticai
Myanmar	Kyat
Namibia	Namibia Dollar
Nepal	Rupee
Netherlands	Guilder
Netherlands Antilles	Guilder
New Zealand	New Zealand Dollar
Nicaragua	Gold Cordoba
Niger	Franc
Nigeria	Naira
Norway	Kroner
Oman	Omani Rial
Pakistan	Rupee
Panoma	Balboa
Papua New Guinea	Kina
Paraguay	Guaranie
Peru	Nuevos Sole
Philippines	Peso
Poland	Zloty
Portugal	Escudo
Qatar	Riyal
Romania	Lei
Russia	Ruble
Rwanda	Franc
Somoa	Tala
Saudi Arabia	Riyal
Senegal	Franc
Seychelles	Rupee
Sierra Leone	Leone
Singapore	Singapore Dollar
Slovak Republic	Koruny
Slovenia	Tolar

Solomon Islands	Dollar
South Africa	Rand
Spain	Peseta
Sri Lanka	Rupee
Sudan	Pound
Surinam	Guilder
Swaziland	Emalangeni
Sweden	Kronor
Switzerland	Franc
Syrian Arab Rep	Pound
Tanzania	Shilling
Thailand	Baht
Togo	Franc
Tonga	Paane
Trinidad & Tobago	T. Dollar
Tunisia	Dinar
Turkey	Lira
Uganda	Shilling
Ukraine	Hryunia
UAE	Dirham
UK	Pound
USA	US Dollar
Uruguay	Peso
Vanuatu	Vatu
Venezuela	Bolivares
Yemen, Republic	Rial
Zambia	Kwacha
Zimbabwe	Zimbabwe Dollar

Appendix 4

Per capita Income of Selected Countries of the World
Year 2000

(in US dollars)

S. No.	Country	Per capita income (in descending order)
1.	Switzerland	38,140
2.	Japan	35,620
3.	Norway	34,530
4.	United States	34,100
5.	Denmark	32.280
6.	Sweden	27,140
7.	Hong Kong	25.920
8.	Austria	25.220
9.	Finland	25,130
10.	Germany	25,120
11.	Netherlands	24,970
12.	Singapore	24,740
13.	Belgium	24,540
14.	United Kingdom	24,430
15.	Canada	21,130
16.	Australia	20.240
17.	Italy	20.160
18.	Kuwait	18.030
19.	Israel	16.710
20.	Spain	15,080
21.	New Zealand	12,990
22.	Argentina	7,460
23.	Saudi Arabia	7,230
24.	Chile	4,590
25.	Poland	4,190

26.	Mauritius	3,750
27.	Brazil	3,580
28.	Malaysia	3,380
29.	Panama	3,260
30.	Turkey	3.100
31.	South Africa	3.020
32.	Jordan	1,710
33.	Romania	1,670
34.	Algeria	1,580
35.	Egypt	1,490
36.	Philippines	1,040
37.	Bolivia	990
38.	Sri Lanka	850
39.	India	450
40.	Pakistan	440
41.	Bangladesh	370
42.	Nigeria	260
43.	Nepal	240

Source: Development Indicators Database, World Bank, April 2002 (excerpted).

Appendix 5
Winners of Nobel Prize in Economics: 1969-2001

1969
RAGNAR FRISCH and JAN TINBERGEN for having developed and applied dynamic models for the analysis of economic processes.

1970
PAUL A SAMUELSON for the scientific work through which he has developed static and dynamic economic theory and actively contributed to raising the level of analysis in economic science.

1971
SIMON KUZNETS for his empirically founded interpretation of economic growth which has led to new and deepened insight into the economic and social structure and process of development.

1972
SIR JOHN R. HICKS and KENNETH J. ARROW for their pioneering contributions to general economic equilibrium theory and welfare theory.

1973
WASSILY LEONTIEF for the development of the input-output method and for its application to important economic problems.

1974
GUNNAR MYRDAL and FRIEDRICH AUGUST VON HAYEK for their pioneering work in the theory of money

and economic fluctuations and for their penetrating analysis of the interdependence of economic, social and institutional phenomena.

1975

LEONID VITALIYEVICH KANTOROVICH and TJALLING C. KOOPMANS for their contributions to the theory of optimum allocation of resources.

1976

MILTON FRIEDMAN for his achievements in the fields of consumption analysis, monetary history and theory and for his demonstration of the complexity of stabilisation policy.

1977

BERTIL OHLIN and JAMES E MEADE for their pathbreaking contribution to the theory of international trade and international capital movements.

1978

HERBERT A. SIMON for his pioneering research into the decision-making process within economic organisations.

1979

THEODORE W. SCHULTZ and SIR ARTHUR LEWIS for their pioneering research into economic development research with particular consideration of the problems of developing countries.

1980

LAWRENCE R. KLEIN for the creation of econometric models and the application to the analysis of economic fluctuations and economic policies.

1981
JAMES TOBIN for his analysis of financial markets and their relations to expenditure decisions, employment, production and prices.

1982
GEORGE J. STIGLER for his seminal studies of industrial structures, functioning of markets and causes and effects of public regulation.

1983
GERARD DEBREU for having incorporated new analytical methods into economic theory and for his rigorous reformulation of the theory of general equilibrium.

1984
SIR RICHARD STONE for having made fundamental contributions to the development of systems of national accounts and hence greatly improved the basis for empirical economic analysis.

1985
FRANCO MODIGLIANI for his pioneering analyses of saving and of financial markets.

1986
JAMES M. BUCHANAN, JR. for his development of the contractual and constitutional bases for the theory of economic and political decision-making.

1987
ROBERT M. SOLOW for his contributions to the theory of economic growth.

1988

MAURICE ALLAIS for his pioneering contributions to the theory of markets and efficient utilisation of resources.

1989

TRYGVE HAAVELMO for his clarification of the probability theory foundations of econometrics and his analyses of simultaneous economic structures.

1990

HARRY M. MARKOWITZ , MERTON M. MILLER and WILLIAM F. SHARPE for their pioneering work in the theory of financial economics.

1991

RONALD H. COASE for his discovery and clarification of the significance of transaction costs and property rights for the institutional structure and functioning of the economy.

1992

GARY S. BECKER for having extended the domain of microeconomic analysis to a wide range of human behaviour and interaction, including nonmarket behaviour.

1993

ROBERT W. FOGEL and DOUGLASS C. NORTH for having renewed research in economic history by applying economic theory and quantitative methods in order to explain economic and institutional change.

1994

JOHN C. HARSANYI , JOHN F. NASH and REINHARD SELTEN for their pioneering analysis of equilibria in the theory of non-cooperative games.

1995

ROBERT LUCAS for having developed and applied the hypothesis of rational expectations, and thereby having transformed macroeconomic analysis and deepened our understanding of economic policy.

1996

JAMES A. MIRRLEES and WILLIAM VICKREY for their fundamental contributions to the economic theory of incentives under asymmetric information.

1997

ROBERT C. MERTON and MYRON S. SCHOLES for a new method to determine the value of derivatives.

1998

AMARTYA SEN for his contributions to welfare economics.

1999

ROBERT A. MUNDELL for his analysis of monetary and fiscal policy under different exchange rate regimes and his analysis of optimum currency areas.

2000

JAMES J. HECKMAN for his development of theory and methods for analysing selective samples and DANIEL L.

MCFADDEN for his development of theory and methods for analysing discrete choice.

2001

GEORGE A. ACKERLOF, A. MICHAEL SPENCE, and JOSEPH E. STIGLITZ, for their analyses of markets with asymmetric information.

Appendix 6
Short Biographies of Famous Economists

Adam Smith (1723-1790)

Smith was one of those 18th century Scottish moral philosophers whose impulses led to our modern day theories. His work *An Inquiry into the Nature and Causes of the Wealth of Nations* (1776) marked the breakthrough of an evolutionary approach which progressively displaced the stationary Aristotelian view.

Adam Smith was born in the year 1723. Adam Smith was to become the first political economist the world had ever known. He was to take his place at the head of the first school of economics, one that continues and is known as the classical school.

Adam's father, who had died before Adam's birth, was a comptroller of customs. In 1740, at the age of seventeen, Smith was sent off to Oxford on scholarship. It was here that he learned Greek and began a sound accumulation of Greek learning. It was here, too, that he read Hume's *A Treatise of Human Nature*, a work written during the years 1734-5.

In 1751, at the age of twenty-eight, Adam Smith became a professor of Logic at Glasgow, and then, the following year, took the Chair of Moral Philosophy. In 1759, he published his *Theory of Moral Sentiments* , a work that spread to both Germany and France, a work that he kept revising right up to his death in 1790.

One, not familiar with his life, might well consider it surprising to learn that Adam Smith wrote his economics as part of his work as a philosopher. One must appreciate that in the days of Adam Smith, much of the study carried out at universities was history and philosophy; a course in philosophy would include a study of jurisprudence. A study of justice leads naturally to a study of the various legal systems, which of course, in turn, leads to the study of government, and, finally, to a study of political economy.

On July 17th, 1790, Adam Smith died at Edinburgh.

Buchanan, James M.

Buchanan, a professor of economics, was the Nobel Laureate in Economic Science in 1986. *The Limits of Liberty* is his famous work.

Edgeworth, Francis Ysidro (1845-1926)

Professor of Political Economy at Oxford (1891-1922), Edgeworth is reputed to be the Father of the mathematical school of economics. Edgeworth is best known for his book, *Mathematical Psychics* (1881).

Friedman, Milton (1912-)

Friedman was born in New York City. He received a Doctor of Philosophy from Columbia. He worked for the US government between the years 1935 & 1943 (US Treasury from '41 to '43). Since 1946 he has been teaching at the University of Chicago. He won the Nobel prize in 1976. He is a believer in the free market system, which will account for his views from everything from the US army draft (he's against it) to monetary policy (floating exchange rates). He is for a negative income tax, and, thus, for the elimination of universal poverty programmes. He is part of a school of economists who associate their views to those of Friedman's. The school is known as the Chicago School of Monetary Economics, a school which stresses the importance of the quantity of money as an instrument of government policy and as a determinant of business cycles and inflation, "monetarism." The Chicago School, is one which has come to its conclusions by the use of the empirical approach, viz., knowledge is gained through the use of the five senses and a process of reflection. Friedman was of the view that minimum wage laws, drug prohibition laws, union monopoly laws, government schools and other welfare state policies exploit poor people. Friedman's written work concentrates on monetary theory, including books such as the *Studies in the Quantity Theory of Money* (1956) and *A Monetary History of the United States* (1963).

Galbraith, John Kenneth

John Kenneth Galbraith was born in Ontario. His first degree was earned in his home province, and, then, turning to the United States to continue with his studies, he was to eventually receive a Ph.D. in 1934 from the University of California. Galbraith was to teach at both California and Princeton before joining the faculty at Harvard in 1948.

During the Kennedy years he was an ambassador to India. Galbraith's works include: *The Great Crash* (1955), *The Affluent Society* (1958), *The Liberal Hour* (1960), *Made to Last* (1964), and *The New Industrial State* (1967).

George, Henry (1839-97)

George was an American economist. His fundamental remedy for poverty was a 'single tax' levied on the value of land exclusive of improvements, and the abolition of all taxes which fall upon industry and thrift. His single greatest work was *Progress and Poverty* (1879).

Hayek, Friedrich A. (1900-92)

Born in Vienna, Professor Hayek was the director of the Austrian Institute for Economic Research (1927-31). Hayek rooted his philosophical thought in Hume, the Scottish moralist, and the English common law. In spite of his belief in liberty and that society could only work if men were free to pursue their own interests, Hayek thought, nonetheless, that government's role extended to conscription, taxes, welfare safty-net programs, and support for the arts.

Professor Hayek, in 1974, was awarded the Nobel prize in Economics. His works include: *The Road to Serfdom* (1944); *Capitalism and the Historians* (1963) and *The Fatal Conceit* (1988).

Hazlitt, Henry (1894-1993)

Hazlitt was better known as a journalist., He began his writing career in 1913 with the Wall Street Journal and eventually became the Literary Editor of the New York Sun in 1925, of the Nation in 1930, and in 1933 succeeded H. L. Mencken as Editor of the American Mercury. In later years Hazlitt wrote for the New York Times and for Newsweek. Though any of Henry Hazlitt's writings deserve a reading, the book that must be read and which will go down on the long time book's list will be his *Economics in One Lesson* (1942). (In this one small volume, written in plain English, one will easily find out all that is needed to come to grips with the subject of economics, a subject which the egg heads in our various universities have torn, much to our misery, completely to shreds).

Heilbroner, Robert L. (1919-)

Heilbroner wrote a most interesting book in 1953, *The Worldly Philosophers*. The book is well worth the read. In his work, Heilbroner deals with the lives and works of among others: Smith, Malthus, Ricardo, Veblen, Marx, and Keynes.

Hutt, W. H. (1899-1988)

A graduate of the London School of Economics, Hutt joined the University of Cape Town faculty where he was appointed Dean of the Faculty of Commerce in 1931. Hutt was a classical liberal economist.

He was to spend most all of his working life in South Africa. He cared not a fig for the vested interests he offended. Hutt attacked the politicians and the Keynesian policies which they adopted for there own use; as far as Hutt was concerned politicians sacrificed principles for expediency. His works include *Keynesianism - Retrospect and Prospect* (1963) and *The Keynesian Episode: A Reassessment.*

Jevons, William Stanley (1835-82)

Jevons is credited with the introduction of mathematical methods into economics. He wrote the *Theory of Political Economy* (1871). His book, *Principles of Economics* came out posthumously in 1905.

Karl Marx (1818-83)

Marx was the German founder of communism. He followed Hegel's deterministic view that all events come about as a result of the inevitable progress of history. With Engels, Marx brought out the Communistic Manifesto.

Marx' prescription was to increase the power of the State. In the process the bourgeois family will vanish along with its complement, capital.

Keynes, John Maynard (1883-1946)

John Maynard Keynes was born in Cambridge, England. His father, Dr. John Neville Keynes, occupied a high level administrative position at the university. Maynard's mother was one of the earliest female students to attend Cambridge. It therefore can be seen that Maynard had a very enriched childhood.

After attending Eton, Keynes went to Cambridge. His first dissertation was on the theory of probability. He was appointed to a position in Foreign Affairs, specifically, the department that extended advice on the administration of India.

As a resultant of a reorganization of the economics department at Cambridge, an opportunity opened up for Keynes (he had earlier come under the influence of its head, Alfred Marshall). And so, Keynes resigned his position with government and went back to Cambridge to teach.

With the First World War having put a huge strain on the British economy a call went out for fresh young minds. In 1915, Keynes was finally offered a job at the British Treasury. Given his position at Treasury, Keynes was to take an active part in the war effort, and, indeed, he was part of the British team sent to the Paris Peace Conference of 1919. The result of the conference was not, however, to Keynes' liking. On his return to England, Keynes resigned his position with Treasury and turned bitterly to writing out his thoughts on the peace process. In the fall of 1919, out came his book, *The Economic Consequences of the Peace.*

Basically, Keynes was of the view that the amount and the manner by which Germany was to pay war reparations to the victorious allies would lead to future problems. Initially, these provisions in the treaty would hamper Germany's post war economy; and, ultimately, it would lead Germany's repudiation of it and a rearming of all Europe.

With the world wide slump, post 1929, Keynes set himself to the task of explaining and of coming up with new methods to control trade-cycles. In the result two books were spawned: *A Treatise on Money* and *The General Theory of Employment, Interest and Money* (1936).

In these books Keynes pronounced that there should be both national and international programs that would lead to a unified monetary policy. Further, Keynes came to the view that a national budget was to serve not only the purpose of good financial planning for government revenues and expenditures; but, that, it ought to be used as a major instrument in the planning of the national economy. What was needed, in Keynes's view, were policies that would regulate the booms and slumps of the trade cycle, viz., that it was the responsibility of government to regulate the levels of employment and investment. He was of the view that economic equilibrium could, and should, be restored and maintained by official action. In such a scheme there was not much room for the classical theory that espoused laissez-faire.

Lutz, Harley Leist

Lutz was Professor of Public Finance, Princeton. In his work *Public Finance* Lutz points out the dangers of deficit financing and makes the case for balanced budgets.

reprinted by Libertarian Press in 1994 which includes an introduction by F. A. Hayek.

Mill, John Stuart (1806-1873).

John Stuart's father, James Stuart Mill (1773-1836) was a close friend of Jeremy Bentham (1748-1832). Together they founded the utilitarian school in philosophy (the greatest happiness of the greatest number). James Mill accepted the theories of Malthus and was a friend of Ricardo; he was an admirer of the French encyclopaedis Claude Helvetius (1715-71); he was a "doctrinaire believer in laissez faire."

John Stuart Mill's education came from his father, and his father's friends, particularly, Bentham.

When it came time to go to work, John joined his father as his assistant at the India House; Mill rose through the ranks to become the chief of office in 1856 and retired with a pension.

John Stuart Mill's great writings were written in his spare time. *On Liberty* (1859) is probably his most famous work. Among his other books are *Principles of Political Economy* (1848), *Utilitarianism* (1863), and his celebrated *Autobiography* (1873) .

Mises, Ludwig von (1881-1973)

Mises was born in Austria. After having studied law, he clerked and eventually became an associate at a law firm. In 1903 Mises read Carl Menger's *Principles of Economics* which profoundly effected him. One of his earlier and expressed beliefs was that universities were but state institutions and the instructors therein civil servants. This view led to a problem that plagued Mises for the rest of his years: the refusal of academia to grant him a full-time, paid position, in spite of his Ph.D. By 1909, however, he had a full time job, one he kept for 25 years, as an economist with the Vienna Chamber of Commerce (which in Austria, is a very influential government body).

He had a terrible time when the Nazis took over Austria and he fled to the United States. His best works are *Socialism* (1932) and *Human Action* (1949).

Quesnay, François (1694-1774)

Quesnay founded an 18th century French school of thinkers who evolved the first complete system of Economics. Being a physician to Louis XV, Quesnay came fully under the protection of the royal court.

He began his economic studies in 1756, when he wrote for the Encyclopédie. His chief work is *The Economical Table* (1758), which he and his followers (the physiocrats) believed summed up the natural law of economy. The physiocrats stressed that absolute freedom of trade was essential to guarantee the most beneficial operation of economic law, which they considered immutable. The physiocrats influenced later advocates of laissez faire including Adam Smith.

Ricardo, David (1772-1823)

Ricardo was born in London. His father was a Jewish stockbroker. With his marriage in 1793, Ricardo turned Christian. He learned well, however, from his father and by 1814 David Ricardo was a rich man in his own right. In 1799 his interest in political economy was awakened by Smith's Wealth of Nations.

Ricardo's Theory of Rent became famous and dominated the science of economics for many years; at least up to the time of Keynes.

Say, Jean Baptiste (1767-1832)

Say was a French political economist. He passed part of his youth in England. He expounded the views of Adam Smith. Say's Law is that ultimately goods and services must be paid for by other goods and services, this truism proceeded his declaration that *supply creates its own demand.*

Schumpeter, Joseph A.

Schumpeter was an Austrian-American economist. His principal work, written in 1942, *Capitalism, Socialism and Democracy* is the classic pessimistic work on the future of capitalism. Since its appearance it has been much disputed by scholars and many of Schumpeter's propositions have since been refuted by world developments. Incidentally, Schumpeter, in spite of the many problems he found with it, favoured capitalism over socialism.

Seldon, Arthur (1917-)

A graduate of the London School of Economics and Vice President of the Mont Pelerin Society. One ought to read Seldon's Capitalism.